With *Kingdom Contours,* Jeremy and Monica Chambers have given us a serious, practical guide to genuine discipleship to the living Christ. I am most pleased with *Kingdom Contours* and highly recommend it to you.

RICHARD J. FOSTER, author of several books including
Celebration of Discipline and *Learning Humility*

Kingdom Contours is a well-written, comprehensive, biblically based, and helpful book for empowering everyday people to shape kingdom movements. This revised edition is even better. I would highly recommend it.

REV. SIANG-YANG TAN, PHD, senior professor of
clinical psychology, Fuller Theological Seminary; senior pastor emeritus,
First Evangelical Church, Glendale; author, *Counseling and Psychotherapy:
A Christian Perspective* and *Shepherding God's People*

In an age of confusion, in which most people do not know what to think or believe, the door to "go and make disciples of all nations" (Matthew 28:19) is wide open—perhaps like never before in our lifetimes! For those of us seeking guidance on how best to respond, Jeremy and Monica Chambers show the way. *Kingdom Contours* functions as a field guide, giving followers of Jesus a generous toolbelt of practices that are theologically grounded, tested, and proven reliable at effectively pointing people to God and making disciples of Jesus. Their approach is intrinsically relational, Christ-centered, love-permeated, grace-based, truth-infused, and multiplication-oriented—just what is needed for such a time as this. Read it! Give a copy to your friends! Join the movement of the Holy Spirit!

MIRIAM DIXON, faculty and board member, Renovaré; author,
Worth Celebrating: A Biography of Richard J. Foster's Celebration of Discipline

Kingdom Contours contains the kind of thinking and action needed to shift the tracks of history in our day. Jeremy and Monica Chambers are well-studied apostolic leaders, and in this book, they demonstrate that they are articulate writers as well. Consider this a viable handbook for a much-needed revolution.

ALAN HIRSCH, award-winning author/coauthor of numerous books on
missional spirituality, leadership, and organization; cofounder,
Movement Leaders Collective, the Forge Missional
Training Network, and 5Q Collective

A must-read resource from two must-know leaders. We're all hungry for revival, renewal, awakening, and movement. This book helps ground those elusive yearnings in concrete practice.

LUCAS PULLEY, executive director, The Underground Network

Kingdom Contours is a groundbreaking resource that has impacted countless disciple-makers across the globe. This meticulously curated compendium features a wealth of resources, intricately organized around six key components of missional movement. It is the quintessential toolkit for equipping missional practitioners and mobilizing the local church for the mission at hand.

In a world longing for movemental leadership, *Kingdom Contours* cuts through the fluff, offering a beacon of guidance and practical wisdom. It is a go-to resource for effectively navigating the complexities of engaging in the mission of God.

TERRY ISHEE, executive director, Forge America; founder, Sequoias Coaching and Consulting; pastor, Restoration Church, Salem

Clear. Thorough. Simplified. Jeremy and Monica Chambers offer a practical guide to thinking about the core components of movement. This handy resource can help get your movement *moving!*

JESSIE CRUICKSHANK, founder, Whoology, co-leader, V3 Movement

A marvelous montage of deep discipleship! Jeremy and Monica Chambers refocus our vision on King Jesus, his colorful paradigms, and loving practices. Trinitarian textures stir our imaginations and motivate us toward more faithful mission. Building on extraordinary research, the Chambers blend their own rich incarnational stories with Christ-centered concepts of contextualization. Enjoy this feast of joyous formational momentum!

JOHN ELTON PLETCHER, lead pastor, Manor Church, Lancaster, PA; author, *Henry's Glory*, *EmotiConversations*, *The Jesus You're Searching For*, and *Your OMNI Year*

Kingdom Contours has impressive depth and breadth of wisdom and beautifully mixes simplicity, insight, and accessibility. All of this comes from the Chambers' years of practitioner experience and leadership insight. This book is a valuable collection of ideas, frames, tools, and exercises for any and every disciple, equipping them to become a seed to unlock movement potential in themselves and the places or people groups God has placed them in.

RICH ROBINSON, cofounder, Movement Leaders Collective and Creo; author, *All Change: Unlocking Kingdom Potential in a World We Weren't Prepared For*

Kingdom Contours is a powerful resource for anyone seeking tools to unlock their missional potential as a leader making disciples who make disciples. Drawing from deep experience and hard-earned wisdom, Jeremy and Monica Chambers offer a personal missiology that is both practical and inspiring, curated to equip readers for meaningful, Jesus-centered mission.

SCOTT STERNER, executive vice president, National Ministries, Evangelical Free Church of America

Kingdom Contours captures something unique and is a delight to read. Many books on missional movements seem full of "answers," but this guide reflects the Chambers' lived-out curiosity and ongoing journey of discovery.

I loved the Trinitarian perspective, which is so vital for twenty-first-century Western culture. We need a mysterious, relational God, and only a Trinitarian God could achieve this. As someone inspired by the Celtic saints, I deeply appreciated the historical perspective *Kingdom Contours* brings. If you are looking for a way to be a contemplative activist who is a missional catalyst, I highly recommend reading this book.

SCOTT BRENNAN, guardian, the Community of Aiden and Hilda

Kingdom Contours is a practical, biblical, and trustworthy roadmap for making disciples and sparking movements. Jeremy and Monica Chambers explore the core DNA of movement thinking and turn it into hands-on tools you can apply to help advance God's work in the world. Their call to move from evangelism to disciplism is exactly what the Western church needs to embody today. *Kingdom Contours* offers the pathway and tools to get you started.

JON RITNER, chief strategy officer, Communitas International; author, *Positively Irritating: Embracing a Post-Christian World to Form a More Faithful and Innovative Church*

Kingdom Contours is a key resource for the church written by two Jesus-centered, people-loving, kingdom-sharing, disciple-making leaders. The insights in this book are not only biblical and needed but also proven and trustworthy. Only read this if you are serious about seeing gospel movement.

MICHAEL PUMPHREY, church planting strategist, Reliant; coordinator and missional coach, The V3 Movement; planter, Awaken Church

Kingdom Contours is a valuable tool that provides the rails for believers to stay on track throughout life's journey. Not only is the book theologically grounded and global in application, it synthesizes scores of timeless concepts from ancient to modern practitioners. Every missional leader will profit by reading and applying this book. It is a rubric to evaluate our effectiveness in striving to fulfill 2 Timothy 2:2.

DR. JAMES AYERS, professor emeritus, Church and Ministry
Leadership Department, Lancaster Bible College,
Capital Bible Seminary and Graduate School

KINGDOM CONTOURS

KINGDOM CONTOURS

FOUNDATIONS, PARADIGMS, AND TOOLS FOR EQUIPPING JESUS MOVEMENTS

Revised Edition

JEREMY CHAMBERS & MONICA PAREDES CHAMBERS

Foreword by **Michael Frost**
Afterword by **Alan Hirsch**

100 MOVEMENTS PUBLISHING

Published in 2025 by 100 Movements Publishing
www.100Mpublishing.com
Copyright © 2025 by Jeremy and Monica Chambers
First edition published in 2020 by Missional Challenge

The authors have no responsibility for the persistence or accuracy of URLs for external or third-party internet websites referred to in this book and do not guarantee that any content on such websites is, or will remain, accurate or appropriate.

Library of Congress Control Number: 2025912224

All Scripture quotations, unless otherwise indicated, are from the ESV® Bible (The Holy Bible, English Standard Version®), © 2001 by Crossway, a publishing ministry of Good News Publishers. Used by permission. All rights reserved.

Scripture quotations marked NKJV taken from the New King James Version®. Copyright © 1982 by Thomas Nelson. Used by permission. All rights reserved.

Scripture quotations marked MSG are taken from *The Message*, copyright © 1993, 2002, 2018 by Eugene H. Peterson. Used by permission of NavPress. All rights reserved. Represented by Tyndale House Publishers.

Scripture quotations marked NIV are from the Holy Bible, New International Version®, NIV®. Copyright © 1973, 1978, 1984, 2011 by Biblica, Inc.™ Used by permission of Zondervan. All rights reserved worldwide. www.zondervan.com. The "NIV" and "New International Version" are trademarks registered in the United States Patent and Trademark Office by Biblica, Inc.™

ISBN (print) 978-1-955142-70-0
ISBN (eBook) 978-1-955142-71-7

First edition cover design by Tony Sorci
Revised edition cover design by Jude May

100 Movements Publishing
An imprint of Movement Leaders Collective
Cody, Wyoming
www.movementleaderscollective.com

CONTENTS

If you want to SEE the book of Acts,
LIVE the book of Acts.

FOREWORD

Michael Frost

Some years ago, I agreed to join two of my daughters to trek the Inca Trail in Peru. It's a forty-kilometer (twenty-five-mile) hike from just outside Ollantaytambo to the ancient ruins of Machu Picchu. Led by local guides, groups typically take four days to complete the mountainous trek through cocoa farms and grasslands, under snow-capped peaks, and into lush cloud forests. We encountered small villages, Inca ruins, rope bridges, and at one point, a river pulley.

A forty-kilometer trek over four days didn't sound too challenging to me. Until I got there. It wasn't the distance I should have been thinking about. It was the elevation. While technically rated as a moderate hike, the Inca Trail involves climbing to 4,200 meters (13,776 feet) along steep, uneven paths, including one carved into the face of a cliff. One member of our group, a German man, had an extreme fear of heights, so traversing the cliff section was hugely challenging for him.

On the third day, as we broke for lunch under a southern beech tree, I asked our guide what the afternoon trek would hold for us. He pointed to a massive peak that towered overhead and told us we needed to hike up that mountain and down the other side to the village where we'd rest that night. I remember my heart sinking. It looked like an impossible task.

It was a stark education in what all those irregular-shaped contour lines mean on a map. The closer the lines the steeper the slope. After all, a mountain range isn't a two-dimensional thing. It has form and shape and variable height.

The kingdom of God isn't a two-dimensional thing either. It is contoured like a mountain range. This is an intriguing idea, one that has bothered me (in a good way) since I read this book. We can sometimes find ourselves speaking of the kingdom as though it is just a set of ideas, or a list of values, as though we merely *think* our way in the good and beautiful life promised by Jesus. But living as those who have bent our knee in allegiance to Jesus takes more than thought. We have responded to an invitation to live and serve under his kingship, and to embrace its demands. It takes all we have but is ultimately only possible when empowered by the presence of Christ himself, strengthening our hearts, softening our eyes, opening our hands.

Speaking of the Christ-filled life of mission as a "journey" has become clichéd but no less true. This following of Jesus involves movement, sacrifice, direction, and courage. It requires focus and resilience. And like all journeys, it necessitates a map, especially for those of us who would dare to lead others along the kingdom's trails toward the summit.

It's for this reason that Jeremy and Monica Chambers have prepared this book like a topographic map of God's kingdom, complete with contour lines to depict the shape of the spiritual terrain we are invited to explore. They guide us through the concentric loop contours that represent the hills and knolls, valleys and dales, involved in leadership in the kingdom. I couldn't help but feel as though each chapter presents its topic as a geographic feature, like a steep mountain or a narrow ridge. All of them are described using three broad contour lines.

First, they survey the lower regions of things like disciple-making, incarnational living, and deep community. The Chambers refer to this terrain as "foundations" and each chapter lays the groundwork for the ascent to higher elevations by outlining how these topics feature in Christ's kingdom. I thought of this as the work of setting up base camp, developing a main encampment to store the supplies needed before launching ourselves up the mountain before us.

Second, each chapter identifies a series of paradigmatic ideas that give form to the topography before us. Then, third, we are invited to choose the tools, practices, or disciplines required to undertake the journey. In fact, the sheer range and scope of practical aids they present in each chapter is quite mind-blowing. Like their previous book, *The Art of Missional Spirituality*, the Chambers have assembled a veritable smorgasbord of ideas, tools, and techniques for developing the kind of kingdom-focused leadership they are commending to us. This three-tiered approach makes *Kingdom Contours* an invaluable manual.

Back to my trek along the Inca Trail: It might go without saying that my daughters and I couldn't have done it without a guide. At times, as we strolled through grassy fields in the lowlands, I couldn't detect any clear path at all. At other times, the ancient path had fallen into disrepair and was difficult to distinguish. But our guide, Daniel, seemed unfazed. He kindly helped our German fellow-traveler along that cliff. He gently placated my doubts about climbing that mountain on the third day. He led us forward calmly and without hesitation. He had made this trip many, many times before.

I find Jeremy and Monica Chambers to be a lot like our guide Daniel. Their book is drawn from years of study, practice, and observation (including, remarkably, three thousand pages of Jeremy's own journaling). They live the things they are calling us to embrace. They are gentle, trustworthy guides. They know the way ahead.

The kingdom of God has contours.

We need three-dimensional charts.

Kingdom Contours is one such map.

PREFACE TO THE REVISED EDITION

Since publishing the first edition of *Kingdom Contours* in 2020, we have received feedback from hundreds of readers who read the book and put it into practice. Although much of this feedback was hugely encouraging, we discovered that the original version wasn't ordered in a way that helped the reader find content quickly, nor was it ordered around foundations, paradigms, or tools as distinctive categories. We realized the potential for a reader to look at a "tool" and say, "Oh, we need to do that now in our church," and then insensitively or inappropriately apply the wrong tool in the wrong context. We therefore wanted to distinguish the difference between foundations, paradigms, and tools. *Tools* can be experimented with and held loosely, but *foundations* are unshakeable, no matter what the reader's context. *Paradigms* act as frameworks, allowing us to address our unique situation with both solid stability and contextual flexibility. In this revised edition, we have sought to significantly improve accessibility by helping readers to contextualize and analyze their situation by referring to paradigms quickly and easily.

It is important to also note what has *not* changed from the first edition. We completely stand by our initial theological views and therefore have not changed any of the theological implications or claims in the book. However, we have changed our tone and aimed for more grace and mercy. We have also revised our wording to encourage readers to engage with the tools and paradigms in an exploratory way, rather than feeling pressured to adopt them dogmatically. (This gentler approach is a direct result of the Lord's grace in our lives, for which we praise him.)

Many readers gave feedback concerning the length of the original book, and therefore we have shortened the content by more than

20 percent by cutting unnecessary verbiage. However, we have not removed any of the critically important details.

Finally, we have strived for a level of excellence in this project. Over the years, we have kept a running list of small changes to improve the manuscript, and as that list grew, it highlighted the importance of a second edition. Given the first edition's wide readership, we also recognized that this book was impacting the personal lives and ministries of many, which impressed upon us the responsibility to enhance the book for even greater benefit and encouragement. Simply put: If you can bless someone even more, why not do it? Why not go the extra mile to create an improved impact? With all this in mind, we hope this revised edition brings greater blessing and empowers readers to explore the kingdom contours of their context more deeply, for God's greater glory.

INTRODUCTION

Since first publishing this book in 2020, a multitude of leaders have read the principles within these pages, applied them to their ministries, and seen a powerful work of the Holy Spirit. So, we have the benefit of publishing this revised edition from a positively reinforced position, knowing that this book's concepts and tools are not only theoretically helpful but proven and demonstrated as being used by the Lord for the furthering of his kingdom.

Yet, a perpetual problem remains: Christians and churches, particularly in the West, continue to focus more on building their own kingdoms than the kingdom of heaven. The metrics we have shifted toward—valuing bucks and butts on seats more than growing disciples and kingdom fruitfulness—create a cycle where we rely on the syncretistic approach of blending church with business/marketing models and tools of "people management." We seem to have forgotten how Jesus did his ministry.

Many Christians who remain heavily invested in the church still fear releasing the old wineskins (church as human tradition or modern corporation). But Jesus offers us lives and communities overflowing with the fruit of love, joy, and peace—his goodness is available to us if we would just pick up his easy yoke.[1]

Globally, numerous "church buildings" are shutting down, and many are questioning whether the church is "failing" or in decline.[2] But is this the best metric to know if the kingdom of heaven is flourishing? Jesus said that not even the gates of hell would prevail against his kingdom (Matthew 16:17–19). And we know the Almighty, unchanging, and eternal God is upholding his bride, despite modern

---

[1] Galatians 5:22–23; Matthew 11:28–30.

[2] Jeff M. Sellers, "Church closures, attacks spike worldwide, WWL 2024 reports," *Christian Daily International*, January 17, 2024, https://www.christiandaily.com/news/church-closures-attacks-spike-worldwide-wwl-2024-reports.

difficulties. The kingdom of heaven has never and will never be in danger of shutting down; God's people are destined for eternal victory.[3]

Despite this promise, we often lose perspective and get caught up in the busyness. So many Christians are moving toward burnout just to keep the machine running. They wonder if there could be something more to church, leadership, discipleship, and kingdom growth. Is it possible for us to experience the type of deep community we read of in Acts? Could we live the faith adventure of the Seventy-Two Jesus sent out? Could we see many people from all sorts of backgrounds coming to know the freeing life that Jesus offers? Could we truly witness multiplication of disciples and gatherings of believers and not-yet believers like we read of in the New Testament and hear about around the world?

Deep down, we all want to be a part of something greater. We long to be on an exciting journey, traversing the contours of kingdom transformation. We want to participate and belong. Jesus invites us to be on this team—exploring and enacting his kingdom. When we follow him, alongside others, we can experience this type of adventure.

DISCOVERING THE CONTOURS OF GOD'S KINGDOM

We have both had the privilege of spending most of our lives attempting to traverse this adventurous expedition with Jesus. Having experienced powerful and intimate encounters with the Lord at young ages, we have pursued theological study and missions experience in church planting and evangelism in numerous countries around the world.

This has included participating in expansive discipleship multiplication movements. During these times, we have continually asked: Why does the kingdom of God have movement multiplication in some places but not others? Why are some generations more prone to certain expressions of Christianity? Why is this Jesus movement so explosive in some places to the extent it is altering the culture of entire countries or demographics while in other places, people consistently reject the message of Christ? What contributes to these expansive movements?

---

[3]   Revelation 21–22.

And what could we learn so that we can harness these things in any place God calls us to?

Simultaneously, we heard many asking the same questions about the early church: How did it spread from a few hundred or so "Christians" after the death of Christ to approximately twenty-five thousand by 100 CE, and twenty million by 300 CE? That is extreme! The more we observed global movements and interviewed spiritual leaders, the more we became convinced that claiming "Christianity" doesn't necessarily imply someone is a follower of Jesus. Quite the opposite. Jesus spoke of how people would claim to do things in the Lord's name, but the Lord would reply, "I never knew you; depart from me" (Matthew 7:23). Our questioning expanded to not only include questions about how to spark movements but also newer and deeper questions—questions of being, questions of integrity, and questions of what it looks like to generate real followers of Jesus who are filled with love, joy, peace, patience, kindness, goodness, faithfulness, gentleness, and self-control. After all, we are told in Scripture that those are the qualities of one filled with the Spirit of God.[4] We began to question how we can work in accordance with the ways that are truly of the Spirit, of life, of light, and of love.

As we led and coached others, we discovered key facets of kingdom movements that ensure they are sustainable, reproducible, and capable of multiplying in all kinds of churches, systems, and people groups. We have grounded all our endeavors in the desire to be truly biblical, honoring to the Lord, and fruitful and transformative. We have also continually assessed if these things lend themselves toward the global movement of the body of Christ. In walking this journey of discovery, pursuing God's mission, making disciples, and asking these questions, we feel as if we have been traversing the slopes of the great mountain of God's kingdom to discover its undulating slopes, craggy rock faces, and sometimes-colossal precipices. Along the way, we have uncovered the contours of this kingdom mountain that are essential if we are to follow Jesus on this great adventure.

---

4   Galatians 5:22–23.

A key text that has influenced us as we've sought to discover these contours has been *The Forgotten Ways*. Written over twenty years ago by missiologist Alan Hirsch, it details his findings from studying movements of God throughout history, culminating in his six elements that he calls "mDNA" (movement DNA).[5] These elements have become essential to us as we have experimented with starting and leading kingdom movements, and they have become some of the key kingdom contours we have returned to time and again. What we share in this book is an unfolding of how these elements can be lived out practically in the life of a Christian community.

Although our discovery of these kingdom contours has felt like a continual fresh awakening, this book summarizes practices that have been occurring within the global church for the past two thousand years! Many books written about these issues describe what our brothers and sisters in the Global South (and increasingly developed nations) have already known and are currently doing in their contexts. Some of the language here may sound new, and a few tools may seem new, but nothing here is new. It is either ancient and has been practiced for two thousand years and/or is already represented globally and latent in the patterns of Jesus and his Word. If you study expansive movements over the past two thousand years, you will see that there have been extreme bursts of powerful activity in various places on and off for hundreds of years—the effect of Patrick of the Celts in fifth-century Northern Europe; John Wesley and the exponential spread of eighteenth-century Methodism; the twentieth- and twenty-first-century global Pentecostal movement, and the ongoing growth of the church in China, Indonesia, the Philippines, Brazil, Peru, and most of the Global South. In studying these movements; we see patterns of behavior that reveal certain elements found in the practices and identity of people in these movements. Many scholars have noticed these behaviors both in history and in some parts of the world today. Yet none of these patterns are new; they are the ancient principles the

---

[5] Alan Hirsch, *The Forgotten Ways: Reactivating the Missional Church* (Brazos Press: 2009).

Lord has revealed to us through the Scriptures. This book examines those practices and offers tools for applying them in our contexts today.

DYNAMICS THAT HAVE SHAPED THIS BOOK

This book is the product of observing over one hundred global church plants and ministries in over forty countries we have served in (including in North, Central, and South America; Europe; Africa; and Asia). This incorporates observations and study of almost every denomination and religion, including analysis of church variances in all fifty states of the US. We have observed disciple-making and church-planting movements that have multiplied to the third and fourth generations—churches that planted churches that planted churches that planted churches! After witnessing such incredible things, we have absorbed this into our understanding of what lends itself to movement-oriented servanthood in disciple-making. This book is also the product of countless people of faith. During the past twenty years, we have interviewed over three hundred spiritual leaders (missionaries, theology professors, pastors, disciple-makers, etc.), gleaning wisdom on certain topics pertaining to the kingdom of heaven and the making of disciples of Jesus. Those insights, themes, resources, and patterns are included here.

We have also experimented and learned while planting, growing, *failing*, and succeeding with over one hundred microchurches, organic churches, missional communities, house churches, other types of larger church plants, and discipleship groups over two decades. As we have pressed into learning and experimenting, we have experienced some of the deepest anguish, seasons of darkness, brokenness, betrayal, threats to life, and attacks on our personal reputation. Therefore, this book is written with great consideration for the universal human broken condition. We know what it means to weep with God's heart for broken and hurting people. This book is the product of those tearful prayers. Yet we don't remain in a cycle of pain but abide in his goodness.

We have also drawn on many works of Christian literature to bear influence on this text; a lot of these books can be seen in the recommended resources section.

As we have observed and reflected on the essential elements found in this book, the Lord has led us to a slower, more contemplative life. It has been by resting in Christ that we have both been born again … *again.* The ambition, obsessiveness, and never-ending whirring of our minds have shifted into learning the practice of stillness and quietude in his presence. Contemplation has become a way of *being* rather than a way of producing/achieving. This has led quite powerfully to many elements we chose to include here. In a similar vein, our trajectory on this journey has been from the metrics of external growth toward internal depth. This means you won't find a plug-and-play toolkit of strategies within these pages. If the contours of the kingdom were that simple, the Western church would have been more successful by now!

Instead, we have found that God often invites us to purposefully disciple, encourage, or equip someone who will never come to "my church plant" (after all, it's not *my* church anyway). We have spent countless hours loving one person as the Lord leads us to minister to them while having to turn down dozens of other people or projects. This has also meant we have turned down excellent evangelistic, leadership development, or disciple-making opportunities so that we can simply sit with Jesus and listen to his heart. Sometimes we have chosen the counterintuitive things because his kingdom doesn't always make sense to the natural mind. And sometimes, we discover new (yet ancient) means of faithfulness, new (yet ancient) means of fruitfulness, new (yet ancient) practices of following him rather than building our own kingdoms and systems.

As we have taken these steps, that sometimes feel scary, we have seen God's movement flowing mightily. We have seen people come to know Jesus in a deeper and fresher way. We have experienced deep community as we have learned to practice the "one anothers" we see in Scripture.[6] There is so much beauty in the kingdom of heaven, but it is messy. It requires experimentation. It can't be measured by our

---

[6] See Jeffrey Kranz, "All the 'one another' commands in the NT [infographic]," *overviewbible. com*, March 9, 2014, https://overviewbible.com/one-another-infographic/.

current metrics of achievement. It requires us to step out in faith and trust Jesus to guide us.

HOW TO GET THE MOST OUT OF THIS BOOK

This book is a guide for those wanting to traverse the kingdom contours. It is less of an instruction manual—telling you step by step which way to walk—and more of a descriptive key to a map—giving you the tools to orient yourself on this journey and discover the kingdom adventure God has for you.

Through practices, tools, insights, and quoted material, each chapter seeks to remove barriers to our experience of the kingdom's movement. These elements aim to help any Christian incorporate the key ingredients for greater movement dynamics in their context.

The outline of this book is inspired by the six mDNA elements portrayed in Alan Hirsch's *The Forgotten Ways*.[7] We take no credit for the outline or some of the terminology. Rather, we aim to honor the goal of *The Forgotten Ways* because we don't see any other literature that so well describes the essential DNA for movement thinking. By DNA, we are referring to the basic core elements or principles that are foundational to movements: Trinitarian and Christ-centered, disciple-making, missional and incarnational in orientation, operating with movemental wisdom, formed by organic structures, and existing in deep community. These DNA elements are found in every single Jesus movement throughout time. If you remove any of the six elements, you create imbalance that restricts a disciple-making movement. Hirsch makes this clear in his writings, so our project is to unpack the elements according to our experience, observations, reflections, additional study, and practice.

Because these elements are designed to be lived out in community, we suggest a great way to read this book is with others. Each chapter contains the same basic components:

Key Ideas: A quick overview of where we are headed and some highlights that you don't want to miss.

---

[7] Hirsch, *The Forgotten Ways.*

See for Yourself: Specific Scripture readings that we recommend for your own study. This is because we are deeply convinced that the Spirit of God impresses his wisdom through his Word more transformationally than through ours.

Foundations: Our unshakable core map, charting the terrain. Foundations provide the rock-solid theological principles that remain constant, regardless of the specific location or context we find ourselves in. They equip and prepare us for the journey, ensuring we have a reliable understanding of the fundamental landscape.

Paradigms: Our guiding compass for contextual insight. Paradigms offer a solid framework, acting like a compass that orients us within our context, showing the possible directions we can travel. They shape how we see and interpret our surroundings, guiding the complex work of application.

Tools: The adaptable, practical methods that light our way. Like a handheld torch, tools illuminate specific areas of need or challenge, guiding our actions. Not every practice will be suitable for every situation. Therefore, careful discernment is crucial in selecting the right tool for the task. Once a particular tool effectively reveals solutions, we can apply it with increasing diligence and frequency, focusing our efforts where they are most needed.

The format across each of the chapters aims to help you to quickly understand the concepts and navigate how you might embody these elements in your context. Our greatest desire is that you go and make your own discovery of these kingdom contours—seeing the incredible way God works through us as his humble servants.

With this in mind, we hope you remember as you read that no matter how you have approached mission and incarnational living in the past, the Lord is calling you to a deeper level of maturity and grace.

As we have shared these elements with brothers and sisters in the faith, some experience great remorse over their previous methods of mission and discipleship. If anything in this book feels like it sets you on a significant course correction, please don't read it with a tone of condemnation. Rather, read these words with a tone and message of grace, and be reminded of the powerful grace of Jesus toward you.

It is by this grace that we can continue a lifelong journey of traversing these kingdom contours. There will always be many more facets of this kingdom mountain to discover, but we are guided by the wonderful example of Jesus and empowered by the Holy Spirit to continue this journey. Let us begin together to follow in his steps.

1

JESUS-CENTERED AND TRINITARIAN
Centering on Jesus as Lord

 KEY IDEAS

- Christ is Lord: Jesus must be central and preeminent in every area and motivation of our lives. Everything good will flow from this first commitment. No kingdom-of-heaven movement happens or is sustained without this conviction.
- Trinitarian: God has chosen to reveal himself as three persons but one being (essence). Neglecting this is to our detriment; embracing this is the beginning of truly knowing him. No kingdom-of-heaven movement happens or is sustained without this conviction either.
- Knowing God *is* eternal life (John 17:3).
- If you want to plant a movement or contribute to his movement in your region, you must begin with the essentials and plant Christ-oriented, Trinity-infused DNA from the beginning.

👀 SEE FOR YOURSELF

Read Hebrews and consider the following questions: What role should Jesus have in your life and in this kingdom movement? How much should you allow a high view of Jesus to pervade your entire being? To go further, read Colossians 1–2, Philippians 2–3, and John 1. How would your life be different if you began to see Jesus as Lord in a deeper way than ever before? What if his love became more of a centralizing force in your life?

Another option is to read the Gospels and seek to see Jesus as he is, questioning how your prior perspective of Jesus may need further development. Ask questions about Jesus' spirituality: What were his spiritual practices? In what ways do you live in the same ways? What did Jesus' mission look like? How are we imitating him in our lives today?

With respect to the Trinity, you may want to pick any of the following passages: Matthew 28:16–20, Matthew 3:13–17, John 1:1–14, John 14–17, Revelation 1, 1 Peter 1, and Ephesians 1. As you read these passages, ask a few key questions: What is evident about the Triune nature of God? What similarities and distinctions are there between the three persons of the Trinity? How did the biblical authors perceive the Trinity to be relevant to our lives? How is the concept of the Trinity important to you? How is this evident in the way you are living?

🗺️ JESUS-CENTERED AND TRINITARIAN FOUNDATIONS

Foundations are our unshakable core map, charting the terrain. Foundations provide the rock-solid theological principles that remain constant, regardless of the specific location or context we find ourselves in. They equip and prepare us for the journey, ensuring we have a reliable understanding of the fundamental landscape.

Foundation #1: Jesus is Lord

Jesus' kingdom movement starts with a simple seed: Jesus himself! Jesus is the seed. Jesus is the life. Jesus is the life within his movement. This may sound redundant, but consider this: God is Love. Jesus is God. God the Father, Son, and Holy Spirit are infinite love. There is no kingdom movement without the Holy Spirit of God flowing through it. No gospel that doesn't involve the Father, the Son, and the Holy Spirit. The gospel is "the power of God unto salvation" (Romans 1:16). The gospel is Jesus bringing the entirety of his love and kingdom to you right here, right now. Jesus changes everything![1]

We cannot begin to talk appropriately about mission, discipleship, ministry, or anything in this universe unless we begin with the One who holds it all together by the sheer power of his will. Scripture tells us clearly that "Christ holds all things together" (Colossians 1:17); he created all things; he is preeminent over all things—in other words, he is to be acknowledged first before anything else. There is nothing in the universe beyond his knowledge or power, so let us start this journey by focusing on Christ, who he is to us, and how we should behold him and experience his love, brightness, and beauty toward us.

Foundation #2: Christ is the "Chosen Face" of the Trinity

Jesus was sent by the Father, came to do the will of the Father, only did what he saw the Father doing, and sends us his Holy Spirit as Comforter and Guide. Over the past two thousand years, people have exhausted their brains trying to understand the nature of a Triune God—three-ness but oneness. How is it possible that God can be three persons but one being? Someone compared the Trinity to the spectrum of light: In white light, there is a range of different colors, but they are all essentially the same—white light. Others have tried to use the illustration

---

[1] The primary aim of this text is not to fully unpack a theology of the gospel, although we dig into it quite a bit. However, for those who want to learn more about gospel theology, we recommend *The Gospel Primer* by Caesar Kalinowski (Missio Publishing, 2012).

of an egg: shell, egg white, yolk—three but one. Which part is not the egg? Which part is the egg?

Yet these illustrations fail to fully explain the *mystery* of the Trinity. The Trinity is not three pieces; the Trinity is not three "facets," as if the differentiation were that extreme; the Trinity is three persons, yet so alike in perfection as to be One in their purest essence. We can try to explain it, but ultimately, we must embrace the Triune Community by faith:[2] God is a Divine Society of three who are all equally perfect in quality that their nature makes them One. If someone could be *perfect* in every aspect of their being and another person could be utterly perfect and flawless, then those two people would be exactly the same in their essence and in their nature: perfect.

Then add a third being just as perfect and you get what we describe as the Trinity. The mystery is too great for us to understand, so the Divine Community sent Jesus Christ to represent, in the flesh, the full Divine Wisdom (Logos/Word) of the Triune God. Jesus is the face and flesh of the Trinity in human form so that we can finally know and understand something deeper about the Trinity.

People sometimes talk about the "God of the Old Testament" as if there is an evil, angry, wrathful God in the Old Testament and then some other God elsewhere with a better mood. The problem is that Jesus said, "If you have seen me, then you have seen the Father" (John 14:9). This means there is no such thing as a Father in heaven who is different from Christ. Many say they like Jesus but not "God." This response fails to recognize that Jesus is God (with the Father and Holy Spirit), and it also underestimates how much the Father resembles the Son. They haven't yet known Jesus well enough to know how much *God* Jesus actually is, and they haven't known God well enough to know how much *Jesus* God actually is. Not only that, but they have not yet known the indwelling Holy Spirit, who is the Divine Comforter to us. There is no part of the Triune God who is *not* the Comforter.

---

2   We will use a number of terms to describe Trinity: Triune Community (emphasizing the unity within the Trinity), Divine Community, Triune God, etc.

If Jesus is the face of the Trinity, then we must study his face, study his life, and learn who he is. Then we will see the Father and embrace the Holy Spirit. All of our actions as disciples will flow from a deeper study of the Gospels to understand who Jesus was, what he did, and *why* he did those things. All our methods of making disciples will spring from this same study of Jesus in the Gospels. Jesus is the face and flesh of the Trinity.

This understanding is vital to grasp as we begin our conversation. We are not leading people to "spirituality" as a vague, ambiguous concept. We are not discipling people so that they can simply follow the human aspects of Jesus, but so that they embrace Christ as the Son of God, One with the Father, and One with the Holy Spirit.

Foundation #3: The Perfection of Love

The Triune God is love—a perfect community. To demonstrate the perfection of love, you need three people. One can love another, but the love is stronger and better displayed when reciprocated back toward the initial lover. Two can love each other, but when two share a common, equal love for a third, you have the initial perfection of all aspects of love: Love toward another, reciprocated, then shared for a third. A friend once said, "For *Love* so loved the world that *Love* gave his only begotten *Love*, that whoever would believe in *Love* would not perish but have everlasting *Love*." In 1 John 4, John tells us that God is love, which means that true love (not superficial) is a miraculous, ancient, and eternal power. We are also told that the gospel is "the power of God for salvation" (Romans 1:16). God pours his divine, perfected, communal love out on us to bring us into community with the Trinity. God is calling a people from human history to be an eternal part of his loving community. This reality lays a foundation for everything to come in your disciple-making and movement thinking.

In his book *Life in the Trinity*, Donald Fairbairn argues that modern Christianity has sometimes forgotten the Trinitarian roots of our faith.[3]

---

[3] Donald Fairbairn, *Life in the Trinity: An Introduction to Theology with the Help of the Church Fathers* (InterVarsity Press, 2009).

We appreciate (and rightly so) the Reformation doctrines (justification by faith, etc.) but forget the deep reality of a Trinitarian-based faith. Fairbairn argues that early discipleship and doctrine merged around this idea of being in Christ and Christ being in God. We see this truth expanded in John 13–17, specifically when Jesus tells us to abide in him and when he claims to be one with the Father. Paul reiterates this truth in Colossians 3:3 when he says our lives are hidden with Christ in God. These truths were essential to the early church movement and early disciple-making. Yet today, most churches focus on how to live a good life or how to apply Scripture to your life (to make it better), and neglect helping people graduate into these deeper realities of life hidden with Christ in God, the abiding life.

Consider this: To know God means that we are transformed by God. As the Apostle John writes, we are changed when we see him as he is; we become like him (1 John 3:2). We are not talking about knowing about God like we might know trivia about a celebrity. The Scriptures exhort us to *know* God. The Psalms are written by men who clearly knew God through the best and the absolute worst moments in life. In making disciples, we are leading people to know God. In being disciples, first ask, "Do I know him?" In knowing God, our faith is sincere, and our devotion becomes pure and heartfelt. The mysteries of his divine nature and attributes are extensive, so we must know and understand him as well as possible while taking steps to embrace him as a child does.

Jeremy was once teaching martial arts when a four-year-old boy, who had only met him once, ran up to him and grabbed his hand, pulled him down, and jumped up into his lap. He laid his precious little head against Jeremy's chest and started telling him stories about his day. This illustrates what the faith of a child looks like. Jesus exhorts us that we must come to the Father with this type of faith! That little boy didn't know for sure that Jeremy was safe, but he had seen enough, and he saw goodness, and he trusted and believed that he was in a safe place, so he came and rested. To plant a disciple-making movement, we must be like that child. Plant seeds of restful abiding in the presence of Jesus.

Anything less will not be sustainable. Let us repent of our secularized hearts. While it is good to have a rational mind, we have allowed our rationalism to far exceed our trust in the Father's goodness. We must come to him as children.

JESUS-CENTERED AND TRINITARIAN PARADIGMS

Paradigms are our guiding compass for contextual insight. Paradigms offer a solid framework, acting like a compass that orients us within our context, showing the possible directions we can travel. They shape how we see and interpret our surroundings, guiding the complex work of application.

Paradigm #1: A Jesus-Centered Movement

After his incredible prayer for the church in Colossae, Paul says,

> He has freed us from the entire realm of the power of darkness and moved us into the kingdom/reign/realm of the power of his beloved Son, in whom we have redemption which is the full forgiveness of all our sins. Christ, then, is the image of God (who is invisible Spirit). Christ is the firstborn or the forerunner of all creation, to be highlighted and exalted above all creation. For by Jesus, all things were created, in heaven and on earth. He created everything that is seen and unseen—even thrones, powers, rulers, dominions, all forces or authorities—*all* things were created through him (by his power and knowledge), and all things were created for him (for his purposes). He is preeminent (placed in superiority before all other things), and it is in his power that all things hold together. He is the head of the body (the gathering of people who have been made Holy by his grace). He is the beginning, the most significant and highly exalted firstborn from the dead (he pioneered the resurrected life for all who would be resurrected), so that in everything, he might be preeminent. For in him *all* the fullness of God (Father, Son, Spirit)

was pleased to dwell, and through him all things may be reconciled to himself, brought back into peace with himself, whether on earth or heaven, making peace by the blood poured out at his crucifixion.

COLOSSIANS 1:13–20[4]

If we believe this passage is true, it should have a significant bearing on how we make disciples. The movement begins here, with Christ being *first and foremost* over all things, Christ being the One who holds all things together. Let us repent of what has turned Christ into a marginal topic in our lives. Consider the incredible Christ-centered nature of the Scriptures. In John 5:39, Jesus says that the Scriptures themselves bear witness to who he is; and in Luke 24, on the road to Emmaus, Jesus shares with the two disciples everything that the Scriptures say concerning his identity. Between those two passages, we see that the entirety of the Hebrew Scriptures (Old Testament) points to Christ. The book of Matthew consistently references prophecies from the Law, the Psalms, and the Prophets that point to Jesus as the fulfillment of each prophecy. In Ephesians, we see perhaps the most potent line of reasoning for us to live our lives fully aware of *being in Christ*. Galatians, Romans, and Hebrews demonstrate how brilliantly the entire Old Testament lays the theological groundwork for Jesus to be the Messiah. This dynamic that Jesus is the key to understanding and interpreting all of Scripture is called the hermeneutical key.[5]

As you consider the people to whom you are ministering and discipling, study through John 1 and Philippians 2. John 1 draws us into a deeper awareness of the mystery of Christ being before all things, being the Creator of all things, being there in the beginning, and being fully God. Here we see Christ—the life and light of humankind, the very being of God, the concentrated essence of all divine wisdom and understanding. The Eternal Logos (Word) of God became fully human

---

[4] This is Jeremy's expanded and exegetically based theological paraphrase, using some phraseology from the ESV.

[5] A good example of a Jesus-centered interpretation of Scripture and theology can be seen in the works of Karl Barth. A diligent student of historic Christian theology may want to look further into some of his writings.

flesh (the face of God for us in humanity) and dwelt among humanity, demonstrating Triune glory, full of and overflowing with the riches and sensitivity of all grace and the power of all truth. Jesus, the Word in John 1, is the one who delivers to us grace upon grace, the effect of grace compounding eternally upon itself. No wonder life and light come to all who believe in him! John 1 lays the groundwork for the rest of the book of John.

In Philippians 2, we see Christ as the ultimate example to follow. We see the humility of Christ on glorious display—for even though he was fully God, he came down and humbled himself as a servant, even to the point of death on the cross. Consider the implications of Jesus' example in the way you lead, serve, and make disciples. Throughout Paul's writings, a solid Christology is central to all his argumentation. In most of his writings, Paul lays a foundation of Christ-permeated theology to unpack an orthopraxy (application toward right living) for the churches. For example, Ephesians chapters 1–3 are Jesus-centered doctrine while chapters 4–6 draw out the application, Romans chapters 1–11 lay a Christ-based foundation for living the realities of chapters 12–16, and Colossians 1–2 lay the Christ-permeated foundation for 3–4. The list could go on. Paul seems to regularly build his case upon Christ as the foundation.

Paradigm #2: Trinitarianism

Many great works throughout church history have demonstrated the beauty of the Trinity, but even then, only in an infinitely limited sense. The early church fathers, Augustine, Athanasius, Irenaeus, and many others, made excellent attempts to describe and understand something that is ultimately beyond our full ability to understand.[6] Yet, to delight in the Trinity takes a less than cognitive approach—it requires the heart.

---

[6] For anyone interested in developing a better understanding of this topic, we encourage reading the many works written throughout church history on the Trinity, several of which are available online as public domain. See the resources section at the back of this book.

To delight in the Trinity means to accept our limitations in understanding three-ness/oneness and to stop and abide in the shadow of the Almighty, to be still and know that he is God, to pause and embrace (or be embraced by) the Divine Community. It also means that as we understand the embrace of the Three/One, we then go and become that embrace to others, for the modeling of pure love toward others is constant in the Trinity.

The primary intra-Trinitarian activity is love. What powerful implications that holds for our communities and our lifestyles! One of Jeremy's first prayers as a child was a prayer to the Trinity. He lay in bed one evening and prayed to Father, Son, and Spirit, recognizing that all three could smile upon him because he was saved by Christ. He was about three years old, yet it was not outside his ability to experience this mysterious embrace of the Trinity as a powerful reality.[7] To embrace the Trinity requires, first and foremost, full engagement and interaction with the Holy Spirit. It is not merely cognitive, although historically we have often limited it to that. Too often in discipleship curriculums, the doctrine of the Trinity has only a few pages devoted to its importance and significance, as if one needs to just "get this part out of the way." No way!

To embrace the Trinity requires the simplicity of what Paul called "walking in the Spirit." John referred to it as "being in the Spirit" (which he was doing just before the revelation from Christ concerning the things to come). Jesus did this on his long walks in the wilderness and in solitude. The desert fathers learned to embrace the Trinity by imitating Jesus' example, utilizing solitude and silence for the purpose of contemplating and entering into Trinitarian reality. Dallas Willard often said that the Great Commission in Matthew 28 tells us to go and immerse people in the Trinitarian reality. All discipleship will bring people into a robust understanding of:

---

[7]   This is a good reason to teach children about these things as soon as possible. Perhaps a child can grasp the reality of the Trinity much better than most adults who get stuck on the details!

- God the Father—loving Abba, who gives good gifts to his children, and protects and nurtures us in his care.
- Jesus the Son—our Brother, our Savior, our Friend, our Head/ Servant.
- Holy Spirit—who dwells in us, leads and guides us, moves upon our hearts with convicting power regarding truth, love, and beauty, who comforts us and is our Helper.

True Christian discipleship brings people into this Trinitarian reality. How could there be discipleship without truly *knowing* Father, Son, and Spirit? In our *being* disciples of Christ, we must love the Father that Christ loved. We must be filled with the Holy Spirit of Christ himself. In *making* disciples, we must introduce people to and then immerse them in the spiritual reality of their true identity in Christ. In light of this Trinitarian reality, we can begin to see a theological center for the entirety of the Scriptures. We call this the "theological center of Scripture." If we take everything into consideration, the theological center of Scripture is the kingdom of the King, who sent Christ so that we can be born again and walk by the power of his Holy Spirit to live and reign in community with the Trinity in his kingdom right now and forever in eternal, overflowing life.

More simply stated, the theological center of Scripture is the rule and reign of the Triune God who redeems. He is a merciful missionary God who sent hope enfleshed for our salvation, bringing us closer to union with him.

Therefore, let us immerse ourselves in his reality and embrace the Triune Community as God present with us! We are hidden with Christ in God, as the father said to the son in the parable in Luke 15:31, "You are always with me, and all that I have is yours" (NKJV). This enables us to live and reign in community with the Trinity in his kingdom right now and forever in eternal, overflowing life. It's all available now, yet with an ongoing crescendo of his gracious power. As Jonathan Edwards noted in *The End for Which God Created the World* and elsewhere in his writings, once we have experienced one million years of goodness, we will have only laid the groundwork to begin attempting to comprehend the exceedingly deeper goodness to come; then after one million more years, it cannot be said that we have yet scratched the surface of the pleasure, delights, and infinite life that he provides.[8] So, in making disciples and planting a Jesus movement, we must learn to *be still* and *know* who he is. In John 17:3, Jesus prayed to the Father and stated that knowing him is eternal life. Jeremiah the prophet said that there is no greater thing to boast in than knowing God (Jeremiah 9:24).[9]

Knowing him requires significant time, energy, and investment in pursuing his ways, reading his words, studying the actions of the Triune God throughout Scripture, meditating on these things, and asking vital questions about who he is, how he wants to relate to us, and who he wants to make us into. We must know Jesus more and more and understand what he did and why he lived the way he lived. Removing the things that hinder us is of utmost importance in this quest. The blinders and idols that stand in our way are enormous, but one by one, they can be removed and replaced with the things above (Colossians 3).[10]

JESUS-CENTERED AND TRINITARIAN TOOLS

Tools are the adaptable, practical methods that light our way. Like a handheld torch, tools illuminate specific areas of need or challenge, guiding our actions. Not every practice will be suitable for every situation. Therefore, careful discernment is crucial in selecting the right tool for the task. Once a particular tool effectively reveals solutions, we can apply it with increasing diligence and frequency, focusing our efforts where they are most needed.

---

[8] Jonathan Edwards, *The End for Which God Created the World* (CreateSpace Publishing, 2014).

[9] As movement resources, we recommend J. I. Packer, *Knowing God*, 3rd ed. (Hodder and Stroughton, 2005) and James Bryan Smith, *The Good and Beautiful God: Falling in Love with the God Jesus Knows* (InterVarsity Press, 2009), which focus more on spiritual disciplines for the purpose of exposing false narratives in our beliefs about God while revealing the deeper truths about God.

[10] See the recommended resources section.

Tool #1: Trinitarian Meditation

Here are some scriptural Trinitarian moments to meditate upon:

- Matthew 28:18–20 is where Jesus tells his followers to go into all the world and make disciples and to baptize (or immerse) them in the name of the Father, the Son, and the Holy Spirit.
- Check out Revelation 1:4–8, and spend some time meditating and praying about the implications for Father, Son, and Spirit. (This passage may raise more questions than answers.)
- Matthew 3:13–17 also provides an exceptional view of the Triune Community. Jesus is on earth being baptized; the heavens open, and the Holy Spirit descends (in appearance like a dove); and the voice of the Father says, "This is my beloved Son, with whom I am well pleased." Luke 3 also affirms this testimony of the manifestation of the Trinity.

Tool #2: Ownership of the Church

Christ owns the church. This may sound like an odd point to put into a section on Christ, but we must consider the implications for our lives as true Christians, connected to the global body of Christ and the local expressions of the gathering of Christ's followers. *We do not own the church!* After all that has been said here, Christ is clearly Lord; Christ is preeminent; Christ owns the gathering. So, as we help others to conform to his image, we *never* own those we serve, and we never own the gatherings that we plant, launch, or facilitate. But this is a common and troublesome phenomenon in the global church. People obey Christ, go and make disciples, and then try to control those disciples. They accidentally teach the new disciples to listen to them rather than the Holy Spirit. Leaders can be intimidated by anything that encroaches on the "power" they feel they have (or think they *should* have).

Jesus said that the best and most amazing leaders would be those who serve others. Jesus himself told us not to be like the leaders of the world (who use their positions for influence or power) but rather to serve. Jesus gave us an example of humility by washing the feet of the disciples. Then, he suffered the ultimate leadership humiliation as he died on the cursed cross.

We do not own those we disciple. We point them to Jesus. We do not control our gatherings, even if we plant them. We point people to Jesus and sow seeds. Jesus said that the kingdom of heaven is like a farmer who sows a seed and then goes and rests (sleeps); when he returns, the seed has grown (Mark 4:26–29). We need to let the kingdom be like that: We should plant seeds and then go rest. We rest because Christ has done the work in us. We rest because Christ does the work for us. Jesus said his burden is actually *not* a burden—it is light (Matthew 11:30). So, let us not take on the sanctification of others as our personal projects. We must be aware that sometimes our positions and paychecks may keep us from experiencing and expanding kingdom freedom. Can we have the courage to pinpoint this in our hearts? Jesus tells us to see ourselves as servants, simply doing our job, and unworthy even to be servants (Luke 17:7–10).

The tool: Carve out some time to pray and surrender those you are ministering to—give them over to the Lord. Prayerfully check and see if there is any sense of false ownership over others or territorial aspects of your heart that need to be given back to the Lord.

A good friend of ours once confided in us about one of her friends who was "trying to convert" her. Then she asked us, "So, are you interested in making me a Christian? Are you trying to convert me?" Our reply was completely honest—we told her we couldn't possibly convert her. It isn't up to us! All we can do is love her, share our lives with her, and share what we understand the truth and the way to be; but ultimately, we cannot control her spirit! This is how it works in the kingdom. We give freedom to others (plant the seed), then we love them (water the seed), but as Paul said, only Christ will give the increase (1 Corinthians 3:6–8). Life comes from him, so we allow him to do the miracles while we become instruments in his hands for "rightness" and righteousness and love.

Repentance from this habit of ownership must take place to release kingdom movement. Leaders must have open hands, not closed fists;

our identity must be rooted in Christ, not in the results of our work. We must release the church back to him on a constant and immediate basis. (This applies to larger groups and individuals you may be discipling.) If *he* is Lord, *he* is building the church, and we can rest in him and obey him in freedom, knowing he does all the work.

IT'S SCRIPTURAL. IT'S RATIONAL. IT'S TRANSFORMATIONAL.

Rationally, even an atheist would admit (and we know some who have) that if you start with the premise that this Triune God is real, then you should logically be about the business of making him your highest, most all-encompassing priority in life. Scripturally, the doctrine of the Trinity (see Jesus' baptism in Matthew 3 and Jesus' dialogue in John 14–16, among others) and the supremacy of Christ (see the entire book of Hebrews, Revelation 1, Colossians 1–2, Philippians 2, John 1, etc.) are evident throughout the New Testament. We have seen the transformational impact of these truths. We have seen thousands of people globally and locally who were infinitely impacted by the realities of the Trinity and putting Christ first. We ourselves are living examples of this.

2

DISCIPLESHIP
Being and Making Jesus-Followers

 KEY IDEAS

- To be a "disciple" of someone means to follow, imitate, and move toward a complete understanding of the worldview and practices of a particular teacher/master. It is *not* simply head knowledge but involves seeking to understand the teacher's heart and perspective. It is *not* merely actions or good deeds but involves imitating the teacher's practices. It is *not* simply being a healthy and spiritually well-rounded individual but being conformed to the teacher's image in an ongoing process.
- To make disciples, one must first be a disciple.
- Being a disciple of Jesus is about really, truly, fully *knowing* him.
- This chapter seeks to provide a range of tools and paradigms for your toolkit to enable you to appreciate the breadth of means for following and knowing Jesus. These tools will enable you to dig deeper and help others to know him. This should hopefully equip you to be a "self-feeder."

- Christ is more concerned with his kingdom than our models of "doing church." To make disciples is more important and more accessible than many of the complexities that we create within our traditions; yet, our traditions can richly and wisely inform us along the journey.

👀 SEE FOR YOURSELF

Read Matthew or Luke and ask yourself: What did Jesus expect his disciples to do/be? What did Jesus model to his disciples? What would it look like for me to imitate Jesus?

To go further, read Romans 12–16, Ephesians 4–6, Philippians 3–4, Colossians 3–4, and 1 Peter. Ask yourself: What do these passages tell me about being a follower of Jesus?

Another option is to read through Romans or Galatians and ask what these books tell us about being true followers of Jesus. How do these books give us freedom?

This chapter has more "tools" than some of the other chapters. Remember, you don't need to use all the tools, but it's helpful to know what's available to you. Tools are meant to be used for specific purposes at specific times. If someone takes a tool and mandates it for everyone else to use, they are in danger of causing harm. (Don't use a hammer when duct tape is needed!) So, prayerfully consider which tools will be most beneficial for you and your context. Then, let the rest stay in the toolshed for later.

DISCIPLESHIP FOUNDATIONS

Foundations are our unshakable core map, charting the terrain. Foundations provide the rock-solid theological principles that remain constant, regardless of the specific location or context we find ourselves in. They equip and prepare us for the journey, ensuring we have a reliable understanding of the fundamental landscape.

Foundation #1: Definition of Discipleship

In the first chapter, we established the value of being Jesus-centered in all things and taking a Trinitarian approach to life, ministry, and discipleship. Now, we shift to the second element of DNA necessary for seeding the kingdom of God: discipleship—being and making followers of Jesus. Since there is so much confusion regarding the definition of "discipleship," let's start with some clarifying factors.

In the time of Christ, people understood that a "disciple" was a particular sort of person with a clear understanding of their identity as a follower of a master or a way of life. In the broader Hebrew and Greco-Roman cultures of the time, what it meant to be a follower (disciple) of a particular teacher (or master) was universally understood.[1] For our purposes, we define a disciple as one who follows the teachings, way of life, worldview, values, and priorities of a chosen teacher/leader.

In the culture of Jesus' day—first-century Palestine—it was understood that a disciple would follow their teacher, obey what they said, and live a life that was intentionally patterned around the central values and message of that teacher's life.

Today, many people pattern their lives around a personal finance guru; a do-it-yourself, self-help blogger; or the values and teachings of a particular philosopher, theologian, "rock-star pastor," or church they read about. We probably all know someone who measures everything in their spiritual life by whether it fits into a particular pastor's or author's set of truth claims—this type of "following" is the perfect example of being a disciple. You can also see a form of discipleship broadly in the general culture with anyone who reads "everything" a particular author writes or listens to "every podcast" or studies "every facet" of some particular cultural trend. People are disciples of too many masters these days. We just trade out the language of discipleship. No one says, "I am a disciple of *this person*." Rather, they say, "I love everything *she* says/writes!" or "*They* influence everything I do."

---

[1] We recommend Bill Hull's works if you are interested in an extended explanation on this topic. See Bill Hull, *The Complete Book of Discipleship: On Being and Making Followers of Christ* (NavPress, 2006).

Discipleship is clearly a general phenomenon all around us. It is a form of deep adoration of a system of truth claims and life practices with respect to one's reality. We all worship something, but we need to become aware of what we are worshiping, intentionally question our motives and hearts, discern why we are worshiping such things, repent (turn in a new direction), and return to worship Christ and his ways first and foremost.

As Alan Hirsch regularly says, "Discipleship is doing the things Jesus would do for the reasons he would do them." Being a disciple of Jesus means we must study his life, constantly asking questions about *why* Jesus did things. Why did Jesus say the things he said? Why did Jesus not say some things in certain situations? Why did Jesus not do certain "good things" in certain circumstances? Analyze his life. Get into the details of how Jesus interacted with people. Dig up the background data on the Gospels and consider the implications of his actions. Ask the Holy Spirit to teach you about Jesus. Read books by men and women who have studied the life of Christ. Find out everything you can about Jesus. Then ask yourself: Do I value the things he valued? Do I practice the things he practiced? Do I pray the way he prayed? And then, after reflecting on these questions, go and live in a way that imitates him.

Foundation #2: The Glory of God

As anyone who has studied the Westminster Catechism will understand, the purpose of knowing God is to ultimately bring him glory.[2] The glory of God is ultimate. The glory of God is all of his beauty and goodness. When you interact with that infinite volume of beauty and goodness, your soul is transformed, elevated, illumined, and nourished in the best way possible. We are made to glorify him and know him. But if we leave that as an abstract concept, we damage ourselves. The eternal Godhead, overflowing with love and goodness, sovereignly

---

[2]   https://thewestminsterstandard.org/westminster-shorter-catechism/. Another great resource, even if you aren't "reformed."

decided to create beings, including and especially humans, that would know, walk with, and glorify the Triune God. Since eternity is in our hearts, we are meant to seek out eternal things (Ecclesiastes 3:11); and the only truly fulfilling, eternal, and most praiseworthy thing is the Almighty Trinity.

Read the Psalms and ask, "What sort of person would say these things?" Read the writings of the New Testament authors and ask, "What sort of people would be so obsessed with these values?" They *saw* his glory, as the Apostle John testifies (John 1:14). To them, the glory of God had been revealed by the Scriptures, infinitely further revealed in Christ, and infinitely magnified by the inner working of the Holy Spirit in their hearts. These individuals look quite different from the sort of person we often see today in modern Christendom.[3]

Foundation #3: Appropriate Order of Discipleship

We must first learn to follow Jesus ourselves before we can help others pattern their lives around Jesus' ways; but the moment someone begins following Jesus, they are already being equipped by the Holy Spirit to help others pattern their lives similarly.

There is a tension here. Some movement practitioners recommend releasing new believers to immediately practice their newfound faith rather than requiring them to take on years of training before they share their faith or make disciples. Consider Jesus with the former Gerasene demoniac (Mark 5:18–20). The guy wanted to go with Jesus as one of his disciples, but Jesus told him to return to his city and tell everyone about his new transformation. Jesus violated many of our modern discipleship curriculums in that moment! Faith, hope, love, and prayerful wisdom will enable you to discern how to balance the tension of sending out disciples quickly and training them diligently and intensively.

---

[3] Historically, there is a rich tradition of writers on the topic of God's glory. Perhaps none wrote more about it than the Puritans, especially Jonathan Edwards. See Edwards, *The End for Which God Created the World* and John Piper, *God's Passion for His Glory: Living the Vision of Jonathan Edwards* (Crossway, 2006).

Foundation #4: Prayer

Robert Coleman's classic *The Master Plan of Evangelism* highlights the importance of teaching people to do what Jesus did, by examining and imitating his life.[4] However, we feel that he could place more emphasis on expectant prayer for divine intervention in this world—something that Jesus did constantly. Jesus demonstrated a worldview that included a Father who hears our prayers and acts directly and intentionally in this world. Jesus also told his disciples to follow his example and do the same. The early church followed him in this pattern and prayed expectantly as they called upon the God who hears and responds. We can also look into church history and see that every century contains testimonies of those who have observed God intervening in the world around them in ways that go beyond the norm. For anyone who thoroughly studies church history, this becomes overwhelmingly evident.[5]

Even Christians who downplay the power of God still pray with strong and overt assumptions about God's sovereignty. Some people claim that God doesn't work in our world or answer prayers, or that prayers only shape "us" but don't impact the world around us. But when the pressure is on, they pray as if they truly believe that he does answer prayers! Many people suddenly discover that they have more faith than they realize when they cry out to the Lord in a time of trial. How we pray tells us something about our underlying theology, even if we don't acknowledge it openly.[6] The same is true of our expectation of

---

[4] Robert E. Coleman, *The Master Plan of Evangelism* (Revell, 1994).

[5] See the testimonies of Justin Martyr, Irenaeus, Tertullian, Antony (by report of Athanasius), Ambrose, Augustine, Gregory the Great, Francis of Assisi, the Waldensians, Vincent Ferrer, Martin Luther, Ignatius of Loyola, Teresa of Avila, an increasing number of communities and churches in the 1600s (and specifically in post-reformation Europe), Jonathan Edwards (and his wife), John Wesley, the Azusa Street Revival, Dwight L. Moody, the rise of global Pentecostalism, and the past two hundred years of the modern missions era. In each case, you see testimony after testimony of answered prayers. See Wayne Grudem, *The Gift of Prophecy in the New Testament and Today* (Crossway, 2000); and John Wimber, *Power Evangelism* (Chosen Books, 1986).

[6] See Terrance Tiessen, *Providence and Prayer: How Does God Work in the World?* (IVP Academic, 2000). This is an exceptional study of this theory and is one of the best books examining how ten theological standpoints impact one's approach to prayer.

active interaction in our world from a sovereign God. We should make disciples who do their best to imitate Jesus. Let's teach disciples of Jesus to ask the Father with surrendered, submissive hearts and bold faith to demonstrate his activity in their lives. Let's teach them the humility to ask and not demand, to respect his timing and his ways, and to pray and never lose heart (Luke 18:1–8). Our personal following of Jesus and our disciple-making practices will be impacted directly by our humility and prayer life.

Prayer is an essential element of all discipleship.[7] Before there was a written Word of God (in other words, in the centuries before Moses began writing the first books of the Bible), there was an oral tradition passed on by people who knew the Lord primarily through prayer. Not long after the Lord showed mercy on the murderous Cain, Scripture tells us in Genesis 4:26 that "people began calling upon the name of the Lord." When you study the patriarchs, you will see that their primary spiritual practice was talking with God—prayer. Jesus spent time alone in prayer, Jesus taught the disciples how to pray, and Jesus modeled prayer.

The prayer book for Jesus and the people of faith in his time was the Psalms. We would do well to learn to pray by spending time abiding in the Psalms. The Psalms free us up to make *all* our requests known to the Lord, to cry out in pain and despair when we are overwhelmed, to rejoice, and to become people of eternal gratitude.

There are many different methods for prayer, but in studying prayer, we would also do well to learn from the prayers of Jesus and Paul (and several others in Scripture). We've read many books on prayer that have left us feeling patronized, almost as if the authors were saying, "One day you will understand prayer, but not until you pray for one million years." It felt as if we could pray for days and hours on end and read numerous books, and yet our prayers would still be limited.

---

[7]   In our book *The Art of Missional Spirituality*, we focus a number of practices around prayer. For anyone interested in embarking on a missional prayer journey, we suggest using the practices in that book as a helpful starting point. Jeremy and Monica Paredes Chambers, *The Art of Missional Spirituality: 31 Sacred Practices for Jesus-Followers* (100 Movements Publishing, 2023).

One book we have found helpful is D. A. Carson's book *Praying with Paul*.[8] Carson draws out the value system in the prayers that Paul prayed and helps the reader to begin to pray in a biblically infused value system. Here are a few examples of Paul's prayers: Ephesians 3:14–21, Philippians 1:9–11, Colossians 1:9–11, and 1 Thessalonians 5:23–25. Read each of these passages. Pray them into your life and the life of a loved one. Look at each prayer and ask, "What sort of person would pray this way?"

Paul prays things like, "I pray that you will be strengthened in the inner being by his glorious riches," that the immeasurable love of Christ will be accessible to your understanding, "that you may be able to comprehend with all the saints what is the breadth, and depth, and width and height of the love of Christ!" (Ephesians 3:14–19). He prays that people will be filled with the "fruits of righteousness" and that they will know how to live in the will of God (Philippians 1:9–11). Paul prays that "the God of peace will sanctify [them] fully" (1 Thessalonians 5:23–24.) Think about that … sanctify them fully! He is praying for *perfect holiness* for the gathering of believers. Paul prays for beautiful, mind-boggling things that have eternal value. Prayer is a foundational element of the spiritual life.

Foundation #5: Gospel Dimensions

Timothy Keller challenges us to consider whether we are embedding the gospel into the way we live and minister:

> It is quite easy to assume that if we understand the gospel accurately and preach it faithfully, our ministry will necessarily be shaped by it—but this is not true. Many churches subscribe to the gospel doctrines but do not have a ministry that is shaped by, entered into, and empowered through the gospel. Its implications have not yet worked their way into the fabric of how the church

---

[8] D. A. Carson, *Praying with Paul: A Call to Spiritual Reformation*, 2nd ed. (Baker Academic, 2015).

actually does ministry. These churches' theological vision has likely arisen from something other than sustained reflection on the gospel. Gospel-centered ministry is more theologically driven than program driven. To pursue it, we must spend time reflecting on the essence, the truths, and the patterns of the gospel itself. It is an unfortunate development within the history of thought in general and the history of the church in particular that has insisted on driving a wedge between theory and practice. The two belong together in a dialogical relationship. Theology here is understood to be … the ministry of Christian understanding— an understanding that aims for the church's fitting participation within the drama of God's redemption.[9]

In order for the gospel to be fully imbibed in our lives, we need to understand its fulness. The gospel is part of the entire meta-narrative of redemptive history: *Creation* in which God made things good; the *Fall* in which Adam and Eve sinned and brought on the curse; *Redemption* in which God provides a way for salvation in Jesus; and *Restoration* in which God is working to finally bring all things into their appropriate and intended place, resulting in eternal restoration—yet God provides the first fruits of that restoration in our lives as soon as we yield to his grace.

As Keller notes, the gospel is *not* so simple that it can be easily reduced to a one-size-fits-all reductionistic line. The Bible *never* gives us something that simple. Jesus doesn't preach the gospel with the exact same terms every time. Look at Jesus talking to Nicodemus in John 3 about being born again, then look at his conversation with the woman at the well in John 4. *Very* different aspects of the gospel are highlighted. The Bible never reduces the gospel but allows it to remain rich, robust, and complex because it is of infinite power. In *Center*

---

9   Timothy Keller, *Center Church: Doing Balanced, Gospel-Centered Ministry in Your City* (Zondervan, 2012), 27–28.

Church, Keller gives us a few themes that we can consistently see in the biblical narrative, to which we've made some slight changes below:[10]

- **Home/exile:** Creation is a place of rest; sin results in self-centeredness, which destroys *shalom*; Israel is exiled; Christ is rejected but breaks the power of death and restores us to the "garden-city" of God. The gospel bears fruit of belonging, peace, wholeness, and completeness.
- **Yahweh/covenant:** We were made for covenant with God, but sin results in unfaithfulness and broken relationship with God; Israel demonstrates unfaithfulness to God, but Jesus takes on the curse and establishes a new covenant so that we may be restored and ultimately invited into the marriage supper of the Lamb. The gospel yields consistency and faithfulness, healing (in all senses, including inner and relational healing), and deep relationship(s).
- **Kingdom:** God brings his kingdom into reality; Satan and humans react and create their own kingdom of rebellion and war, resulting in enslavement; Israel is always longing for a true king; Jesus returns as the true King who frees us from the world, flesh, and the devil; then Christ brings restoration and true freedom under the reign of God. The gospel brings true empowerment, identity, purpose, belonging, and freedom.

These are just three examples of gospel fluency. Each example reveals something deeper about what our hearts are longing for: home (rest), covenant (security), and kingdom (belonging/identity). Gospel fluency happens when we begin to see the gospel influencing every area of our lives.[11]

---

[10] Keller, *Center Church*, 41–43.

[11] See Neil T. Anderson, *Living Free in Christ: The Truth About Who You Are and How Christ Can Meet Your Deepest Needs* (Regal Books, 1993). In this classic, Anderson goes over dozens of angles of how the gospel must touch each area of our identity.

DISCIPLESHIP PARADIGMS

Paradigms are our guiding compass for contextual insight. Paradigms offer a solid framework, acting like a compass that orients us within our context, showing the possible directions we can travel. They shape how we see and interpret our surroundings, guiding the complex work of application.

Paradigm #1: Evangelism as a Subset of Discipleship

Often, churches, denominations, church-planting networks, and mission agencies put evangelism first and speak about discipleship as coming (logically) after evangelism. This is their line of reasoning: (a) share the gospel with people outside the faith (evangelism), (b) they put their faith in Jesus, (c) we "disciple" them (teach them the ways of Jesus). It seems like a logical order. But a deep problem here leads to many of the problems those organizations currently face and have historically experienced. They put the cart before the horse.

Biblically defined evangelism is a gift that is a product of being a follower of Jesus. It is given by the Holy Spirit for the purpose of building up the body of Christ and bringing the gathering of believers to maturity. Evangelism belongs inside *and* outside the church. Those inside the church *need* the good news preached to them by those who are gifted in evangelism. Those outside *also need* the good news preached to them.

If we focus on making disciples of *everyone* around us, we are constantly offering opportunities for anyone and everyone to take steps closer to Jesus. This means that evangelism happens in its proper time, as the Holy Spirit leads us. We must be "gospel fluent"—where we allow the good news to permeate every aspect of our lives. We can become so full of the good news of Jesus that our lives are permeated with goodness, hope, love, and joy.[12] Gospel fluency must be both a

---

[12] Soma Communities and Jeff Vandersteldt speak of this. See "About," Soma Churches, https://www.wearesoma.com/about; and Jeff Vandersteldt, *Gospel Fluency: Speaking the Truths of Jesus into the Everyday Stuff of Life* (Crossway, 2017).

lifestyle and an intentional practice. Evangelism is not just a gift; it is also an extremely powerful spiritual discipline that transforms the person who is sharing the good news. Evangelism has the potential to shape both the speaker and listener into the image of Christ.[13]

At what point were the disciples saved? Perhaps Nathanael entered immediately into saving faith in Christ after his first encounter with Jesus in John 1; perhaps Peter didn't connect the dots until he proclaimed Christ as the Son of God in Matthew 16; perhaps Thomas didn't have "saving faith" until he proclaimed, "My Lord and my God!" in John 20:28. But how can we know? All we know is this: Jesus asked these guys to follow him, then discipled them *constantly* through his way of life, while always proclaiming the good news of the kingdom (evangelism) to them and to the crowds. Jesus' form of evangelism comes under the umbrella of his lifestyle of making disciples. It seems evident then that we should follow Jesus and his way of evangelism and making disciples. Discipleship must encompass all dimensions of our lifestyle. We must become disciple-makers who constantly allow the overflow of his good news and love in our lives to spill onto everyone around us.

Reversing this order creates unnecessary tensions. If we put evangelism first and discipleship second, we create a bifurcation between the two. Evangelism is not pitted against discipleship (or vice versa). And discipleship is not a subset of evangelism; rather, evangelism is a subset of discipleship. As we make disciples, we proclaim the good news of the kingdom throughout the entire process. The highest goal of a disciple is to know Jesus first before making disciples.

It's necessary to understand how spiritual gifting impacts making disciples. Christians aware of the gifts of the Spirit often focus on one gift over others. In Romans 12, 1 Corinthians 12, Ephesians 4, and 1 Peter 4, all sorts of gifts are evident with various purposes, manifestations, and callings. Yet, every gift is a result of being a follower of

---

13 If it is difficult for you to grasp this idea of the need for evangelism both inside *and* outside the body of Christ, we encourage you to read Alan Hirsch's *Disciplism: Reimagining Evangelism Through the Lens of Discipleship*, 2nd ed. (100 Movements Publishing, 2023).

Jesus and receiving these gifts by his Spirit. For example, if one focuses only on the gift of hospitality, one may eventually train one's life in the direction of using this gift without focusing on making disciples.

However, if the focus is first on making disciples, then one learns to make disciples using the gift of hospitality, and this gift is employed appropriately. The same goes for any other gift. Christians easily become imbalanced when we focus more on our giftedness rather than simply following Jesus. These imbalances can easily compound over time with negative consequences.[14]

Paradigm #2: Three Historical Approaches to Discipleship

Many of Bill Hull's books are refreshingly deep and comprehensive, especially *The Complete Book of Discipleship*. Hull identifies three historic and global aspects of discipleship.

- **Classic discipleship**—curriculum/obedience/accountability/ information-oriented discipleship—has benefited many and had its place, but it has sometimes been disconnected from deeper heart transformation at the cost of focusing on external forms of godliness.
- **Spiritual formation**—the historical practices of transforming the inner person and denying the flesh for the purpose of growing in intimacy with Christ. When used alone, this approach can lead to disconnection from orthodoxy, a focus on legalism, and undermine the importance of right teaching; yet it has also led many toward deeper places of walking with Jesus than ever before.
- **Environmental discipleship**—corporate (communal/body of Christ) growth as a key to following Jesus. We do not only follow

---

[14] Along these lines, we recommend Andy Stanley, *The Principle of the Path: How to Get from Where You Are to Where You Want to Be* (Thomas Nelson, 2011); and Darren Hardy, *The Compound Effect: Multiply Your Success One Simple Step at a Time* (Vanguard Press, 2010). These books illustrate that how you set up your life now will have huge effects in the future (good or bad).

Jesus by a knowledge and obedience orientation (classic discipleship), or by practicing rituals to pursue Jesus by denying the flesh and forming the inner person (spiritual formation), but also by following Jesus in community together. This third approach helps to invigorate the other two. This togetherness, a secret of discipleship that perhaps the early church understood much better than anyone else in church history, is making a comeback in transforming our rhythms of followership today.

Hull claims that the merger of these three, while having the potential to create healthier disciples, must also demonstrate its efficacy by transforming the lost around the world; otherwise, it could be seen as just another trendy theme in "discipleship."[15]

Which of these three approaches to discipleship has influenced you the most? Can you spot any personal imbalance toward one or two of the three? How might you move toward more holistic discipleship?

Paradigm #3: Six Streams (Dimensions) of Historic Christianity

In his book *Streams of Living Water*, Richard Foster identifies six dimensions of historic and current Christianity.[16] Depending on your background, you may have been significantly influenced by one or two of these dimensions. You may even feel uncomfortable with a few of them, yet each of these six is seen in the life of Christ and church history:

- **Biblical/Evangelical:** focusing on Scripture, Jesus, and communicating the gospel.
- **Holy Spirit/Charismatic:** oriented around and attentive to the things pertaining to the activity of the Holy Spirit.

---

[15] Hull, *The Complete Book of Discipleship*, 20.

[16] Richard Foster, *Streams of Living Water: Celebrating the Great Traditions of Christian Faith* (Hodder and Stoughton, 2019).

- **Holiness/Virtue:** aiming toward a life that exemplifies and practices the beauty of God's holiness.
- **Prayer/Contemplative:** grounding the spiritual life on the foundation of prayer, quietness, self-control, and becoming aware of the inner workings of the Lord.
- **Incarnational/Sacramental:** highlighting the value of tangible representations of the goodness and mystery of God.
- **Compassion/Justice:** practicing a lifestyle of care, love, and attention to those who are hurting, with a special focus on bringing freedom and healing.

Each of us could easily allow these dimensions to shape us in an imbalanced manner. We could judge other Christians and condemn them for not "praying enough" or not being "biblically correct," etc. We have all seen what happens when a person is leaning too much on one of these six dimensions. Imagine the compassion/justice-oriented person becoming hostile toward others to overcompensate for injustices in the system; or imagine the person delivering doctrinally dead Bible studies that yield no fruit; or imagine the charismatic who gets just a little bit too removed from that which is biblical. *We need a discipleship that is informed by all six dimensions of Christianity.*[17]

Paradigm #4: Sacred Pathways

In his book *Sacred Pathways*, Gary Thomas identifies nine different discipleship pathways that people tend to follow within the Christian tradition.[18] He identifies these tendencies as products of internal temperament, predisposition toward various practices, and seasonal factors or circumstantial events in a person's life. Some people will find certain pathways to be beneficial and spiritually invigorating, while other pathways may feel tedious and even extremely uncomfortable.

---

[17] We recommend reading through Foster's book *Streams of Living Water* as a starting point for reconstructing a more robust approach to discipleship.

[18] Gary Thomas, *Sacred Pathways: Discover Your Soul's Path to God* (Zondervan, 2000).

If the body of Christ could begin to understand our internal diversity, then we would actually appreciate these differences instead of judging others for growing in different ways to us. The insights from this paradigm also enable us to discern where we have been and where we may personally be headed as we go through various seasons and transitional points in our lives. We describe the nine pathways as follows:

- Finding God in nature
- Finding God through the senses
- Experiencing God through ritual and symbols
- Loving God with solitude and simplicity
- Loving God by engaging in a form of activism
- Loving God by caring for others
- Experiencing God through mystery and celebration
- Loving God through contemplative living
- Loving God with the mind

Paradigm #5: Semi-Monasticism[19]

It is vital that everyone learns a cadence of pursuing the Lord that works for them and enables them to *know* God in the stillness of being in his presence while still being actively involved in the world around them. We don't need to describe how extremely un-contemplative our current culture is or how distracted and overstimulated our modern information age and socially maximized culture has become. The ancient pathway to peace is laid out in the Psalms, followed by the Prophets, and illustrated in the rhythms of Jesus' life, the lives of the disciples who followed him, and the early believers. Throughout church history, there have been people who have taken intentional steps to move to places of isolation for the purpose of pursuing and knowing the Lord. While we don't recommend asceticism as a form of reactionism, we do

---

[19] We see semi-monasticism as bolstered and equipped by practicing both the missional outward activist life and the inward life of a contemplative. Our book *The Art of Missional Spirituality* aims to equip practitioners to engage in both of these life orientations in a blended and well-informed manner.

recommend a semi-monastic practice that will enable you to *see* the world around you, *rest* in him, *be* who he is forming you to be, *delight* in him, *enjoy* what he has given you, and *know* his love:

- *Divert yourself daily* for the purpose of connecting deeply with him.
- *Withdraw weekly* from activity (as a Sabbath) for the purpose of resting in him and gaining perspective.
- *Annually abdicate* all responsibility for at least a few weeks in order to release yourself from an achievement-oriented identity and find your true identity in Christ.[20]

Paradigm #6: On the Making of a Disciple

Another brilliant tool in making disciples is Robert Clinton's incredible book on discipleship: *The Making of a Leader*.[21] He speaks of phases and processes that bring about maturity in a disciple-maker's life.[22]

Over the course of our lives, we move from early to mid to later ministry phases. Clinton says each phase involves "process items," which are the elements that impact how we grow. We can have positive or negative experiences of these process items (e.g., family, school life, mentoring, ministry/mission experience, etc.). How a person engages with these process items determines whether they mature.

It is beneficial for us as disciples to see where we are in these stages. Understanding these stages also helps us to be patient with those we

---

[20] See Mark Buchanan, *The Rest of God: Restoring Your Soul by Restoring Sabbath* (Thomas Nelson, 2006); Eugene Peterson, *The Contemplative Pastor: Returning to the Art of Spiritual Direction* (Baker, 2004); Shelley G. Trebesch, *Isolation: A Place of Transformation in the Life of a Leader* (Barnabas Publishing, 1997); Jerome Daley, *Gravitas: The Monastic Rhythms of Healthy Leadership* (NavPress, 2020); and Henri Nouwen, *In the Name of Jesus: Reflections on Christian Leadership* (Darton, Longman and Todd Ltd, 1989).

[21] Robert Clinton, *The Making of a Leader, Recognizing the Lessons and Stages of Leadership Development*, 2nd ed. (NavPress, 2012).

[22] Clinton describes a "maturing" process as having three major movements (Early Ministry, Mid-Ministry, Later Ministry) and four smaller sub-phases (Entry to Ministry, Training in Ministry, Relational Learning, and Discernment).

are discipling—although we would encourage you to use this as a tool or reference rather than as a rigid process.

Even the most challenging of the process items are opportunities for growth. Secular psychologists note the neurological effects of "thinking about the future" when going through hard times; the mind begins to replenish appropriate chemicals when there is a future orientation. For followers of Jesus, going through a trial can help us push through to see what future opportunity it may bring for serving our King. Robert Clinton points out that when leaders know this, they see process items as special and appointed opportunities for growth in depth, wisdom, understanding, love, compassion, strength, and so forth.

Process items can also include ministry tasks/challenges that people move through as they enter kingdom servanthood. These may be as simple as learning to share a testimony, pray out loud, speak in front of a group, serve behind the scenes, take on the challenge of explaining one's faith to a younger person of faith, take on the ministry challenge of praying for someone in need, etc. These enable a disciple-maker to encourage those they disciple to step toward the next level of more intentional development.

As followers of Jesus continue to grow, there are seasons (or "phases," as Clinton calls them) of life where an individual must learn new lessons and process various types of trials. These phases include a training phase where a person is learning, an implementation or ministry activation phase where the individual is doing the hard work of ministry, and a relational phase where they are growing beyond mere actions to engaging the Lord in the depths of their heart.

Clinton says that as an individual goes through this relational phase, they may experience ministry conflicts that hone their growth and may also see leadership backlash (where people take offense at their leadership or purposefully subvert their ministry by gossiping, attacking, etc.). These experiences can seem soul-crushing. This is when a disciple-maker must learn to identify with Christ, to share in his sufferings (Philippians 3:10), to learn from his loving correction (Hebrews 12), and to grow in wisdom in deeper ways than ever imagined. These trials are what Crawford Loritts refers to as the "gems of leadership" in his incredible book *Leadership as an Identity*. For the one who presses on through these things, there is a maturing phase where deepening wisdom, love, prayer, and faith become more apparent.

We must cultivate such a profound love and desire for intimacy with Jesus that trials are welcomed with great joy for the sake of the growth they enable. Read, pray, and meditate on James 1:2–4, Romans 8, and 2 Corinthians 1. Contrast the mindset of the human authors of these passages with your mindset. Is the way of thinking in these passages foreign to you? If so, what type of perspective would make someone joyful in a trial? We can personally attest to the power of these passages and the transformational joy that comes once this perspective is embraced.

Clinton observes that anyone can stay stuck at one of these phases or move forward. Consider what God is asking both you and those you disciple to respond to in order that you can mature in the phase you/ they are at.

Paradigm #7: On the Critical Journey

Janet Hagberg and Robert Guelich speak about moving beyond a "productive ministry" stage of life toward a more inward journey— the journey of identifying and working through motives, dealing with hurts from the past, beginning to see Jesus heal your deepest pains, and moving from understanding your identity in Christ as simply a cognitive set of ideals to seeing those ideals as true holistic transformation.[23] Some Christians experience an intense, life-altering season that leads them to cut ties with their former ideals and/or motivations that were unhealthy or less grounded. Upon a deep and wise transition out of this great trial, many mature Christians report embracing a more outward journey to ministering to others. Some even begin to experience a willingness to serve in unique ways that may cause them great pain—willingness to serve with confidence no matter the

---

[23] Janet O. Hagberg and Robert A. Guelich, *The Critical Journey: Stages in the Life of Faith* (Sheffield Publishing Company, 2005).

backlash—and greater confidence in the Lord's love and power at work through them, even to the point that they look quite odd and frustrating to people who are at earlier stages of growth. This is ultimately for the purpose of leading us into deeper love, wisdom, peace, and joy than ever before; the fruits of the Spirit become an infinite reality as the Holy Spirit guides and transforms our lives.

The journey we often see people take is as follows:

1. Entering into faith with a basic awareness of God
2. Progressing to an information-based form of discipleship (gaining appropriate knowledge and biblical and theological thought structures)

(These first two lead to more productive ministry but are mainly mind-oriented discipleship that falls short of heart transformation.)

3. An inward journey, learning to surrender the heart and all areas of life to Jesus and his sanctification
4. Further stages of increasingly deeper intimacy with Christ and the realization of love as an all-encompassing reality in life

Do your typical discipleship structures enable people to move beyond mere informational discipleship? Does your church have the tools and systems to help people go deeper in their relationship with Christ? Are your systems and processes simply bringing people to information-oriented discipleship and productive ministry without the deeper realities?

Paradigm #8: Covenant and Closed Community

While we will explain this point further in chapter six on Deep Community, it is helpful to touch on it now. Bill Hull makes some excellent points in *The Complete Book of Discipleship* about covenanting together in community to be a people committed to one another on the journey toward Christlikeness.[24] In our consumer Christian

---

[24] Hull, *The Complete Book of Discipleship*, 231.

culture in America, we see people frequently jumping from one church to another, from one group to another, never learning to love with relational endurance, to build relational equity in perseverance with one another, or to increase the power of a relationship through mutual forgiveness. The ancient command to "bear with one another" in Colossians 3:13, with the understanding that love "bears all things," is something that is lost in the consumer orientation of those who look for a church that "feeds" them or gives them what they want. When we have this mindset, we lose the ability to see our belonging in the body in relation to our willingness to love and sacrifice for others.

Church isn't about what you get from it but about being the people of God together, in line with his heart. Church as an enterprise or industrial complex or as a modern corporation has blinded us *by its very structure* to these realities.[25] Pastors wonder why they can preach endlessly about certain kingdom-of-heaven realities yet never see the fruit. Perhaps they need to question the structure and form of their church and see if it is actually promoting the fruit of consumer culture. This is not to say that we need to eliminate certain forms of church. It just means that every church must periodically ask questions regarding the faithfulness and fruitfulness of their form. We *do* need a wide range of forms of church—this represents the beauty of the diversity of the body of Christ. When people covenant together, it creates continuity, safety, and trust, allowing people to struggle within the confines of love together.[26]

Paradigm #9: Dimensions of Spiritual Growth

Jesus is the Author and Completer of our faith. The Holy Spirit is in charge of our sanctification and spiritual growth. Numerous theologians throughout church history have pointed to the means by which

---

[25] JR Woodward and Dan White Jr. highlight this point in *The Church as Movement: Starting and Sustaining Missional-Incarnational Communities* (InterVarsity Press, 2016), 25.

[26] See Dietrich Bonhoeffer, *Life Together: The Classic Exploration of Faith in Community*, 5th ed. (HarperSanFrancisco, 2009); and Larry Crabb, *The Safest Place on Earth: Where People Connect and Are Forever Changed* (W Pub Group, 1999).

the Spirit will cause us to grow, if we are willing and cooperative with his work in our lives. For the follower of Jesus who is lovingly intent on growing closer to the Lord, there seems to be three primary means by which the Spirit helps us to grow: time (the flow of normal life), trials, and spiritual disciplines. Time and trials will happen to us no matter what, but we have intentional control over how we approach spiritual disciplines. Indeed, it is the practice of spiritual disciplines that also enables us to respond to the passage of time and trials with grace and godly character.

We believe that we can utilize the historic spiritual disciplines as a means of targeting various dimensions of our spiritual life in order to directly promote and stimulate spiritual growth. However, we say this with the assumption that we are fully dependent on the work of the Holy Spirit, and therefore cooperating, by faith, with the Spirit. Said differently, it is all grace that we rely upon. If we were to use some simple disciplines such as prayer, Bible study, silence and solitude, journaling, fellowship/spiritual friendship(s), and orient those disciplines around the following aspects, then we could target areas of our lives that may be in need of additional strengthening.

Here is a partial list of various compelling spiritual disciplines to focus on as key aspects of the spiritual life:

The relational dimensions of love. We love God fully, love ourselves appropriately, and love others sincerely. All of life can eventually be seen through a lens of love. We are loved perfectly, and because of this perfect love from the Father we can be filled as deeply as we need with his love, and then we can flow outwardly in love toward all others.

Eternal perspective. We leave behind the limited temporal perspective of only having one life, and we pick up the reality that we are made with eternity in our hearts (Ecclesiastes 3:11) and have an unending destiny ahead of us. This changes how we approach life, trials, and others. We also become aware that Scripture informs us that there are additional eternal rewards for those who seek the kingdom in all things (2 Corinthians 5:10).

Identity in Christ. Once we understand the true nature of what Jesus has done for us, it can open us up to the overwhelming transformative power that comes from knowing our true identities as new creatures, born again.

Biblical motivators. The Bible gives us many interesting and diverse incentives for living in particular ways. Our motivations can be more and more conformed to God's motivations to compel us toward action/being. Some of those motivations include love, gratitude, eternal rewards, identity, purpose, hope, longing for God, etc.

Holistic integration. If we take periodic inventory of every aspect of our lives, we can easily find areas that are yet to be healed, yet to be conformed to his image, yet to be freed. It benefits us to look for areas that we may need some help or additional grace in and ask key questions about how we can surrender these areas to Jesus and continue to strengthen the areas of weakness (Hebrews 12:12). Holiness is truly becoming who the Lord has intended us to become, so as we look at areas where we are not fully healed, we discover ways that the Lord is leading us to be transformed.

Attention to the process. This is a journey of becoming, not simply doing. The Lord invites us to be transformed in an ongoing way. This requires patience and perspective. Reflection, journaling, spiritual friendships, and examination can help us to see how the Lord is at work within us over a long period of time.

Walking by the Spirit. It is one thing to acknowledge that there is a Holy Spirit; it is another to live a life continually engaged in abiding in the Spirit of Jesus. This simple paradigm that Jesus invites us to (abiding: John 14) and Paul reinforces (walking: Galatians 5:16) is one that can take a lifetime to practice; it is truly a craft that we are invited to live into.

Spiritual warfare. In many circles, the reality of spiritual warfare is neglected or dismissed, but for those who are attentive, the clash of the kingdoms is evident. In our global travels, we have seen and experienced true spiritual realities and warfare that can only be described adequately in biblical terms. Ephesians 6:10–20 puts it all in perspective—our struggle and our war is not against flesh and blood. We are not waging war against *humans* but against spiritual forces of wickedness. If we can truly grasp this and the host of other passages that emphasize this aspect of our spirituality, we will begin to experience his power in ways that we would never have imagined. This is a vital part of making disciples. Just look at the ministry of Jesus: How often did he deal with spiritual realities? Do we consider these realities in our day?

Body life. Spiritual formation is not meant for isolation but to be practiced in community within the body of Christ. In Philemon verse 6, Paul prays that Philemon would know every single good thing that he has in Christ through the sharing and fellowship of his faith. This single verse gives us extraordinary insight: It is in the sharing of mutual faith with others that we can experience the depths of just how much we have in Jesus. We think this verse also includes an evangelistic component where in the very sharing of our faith, we are opened up to deeper realities of what we actually have in Jesus.

Missional spirituality. This is the aspect of our spirituality that is significantly edified when we engage in the mission of God. This is where we begin to see our gifts activated as we look to put ourselves in service to the King and his kingdom. It is here where we recognize that the Father sent the Son, and the Son sends us, so God is a sent and sending God. Our Christology reveals to us that Jesus is sent forth but also sends us forth. Therefore, our Christology should influence our missiology (we are sent), and this has implications for all other components of our lives—wherever we are, we are sent forth to be ambassadors for Christ, as 2 Corinthians 5 informs us. This leads us to a strategic mindset informed by the direct teachings, parables, and life of Jesus. Multiplication is a vital part of his strategy and should be a vital part of our way of life.

It's important to take a closer look at the concept of "missional spirituality." Missional spirituality is deeply concerned with the expansion of the kingdom while simultaneously resting patiently in the Lord's timing and embracing the mysterious nature of the kingdom. Missional spirituality can be counterintuitive at times, e.g., praying may seem ineffective to the world, yet is hugely fruitful in the spiritual realm. Engaging with missional spirituality requires us to ask some key questions about the strategic value of our disciple-making: Am

I teaching disciples anything that seems good but is actually unnecessary to his kingdom? Am I distracting people with practices that inhibit them from becoming who they need to be? (Sometimes, our churches lack spiritual strategy because we teach all sorts of things that are irrelevant to who believers need to become in Christ.)

Missional spirituality is heavily influenced by *being* in God's presence. This spirituality understands that we don't need to rush; we can be still and allow him to take as much time as he wants to shape us so that when he calls us to give away our time, energy, etc., we are giving out exactly what he wants. This type of patience understands why Joseph was in prison for all those years, why Moses waited in the wilderness for decades, why Jesus spent less than one tenth of his earthly life in public ministry, why Paul had so many years pass before he was finally sent on his missionary journeys, why Abraham waited so long to see the beginnings of God's promise, why God allowed Isaac and Jacob to "waste" so much of their lives, why David spent such a long time in the wilderness before becoming king, why the prophets suffered, why John the Baptist was beheaded *while* Jesus was on earth, why Jesus washed the feet of the disciples, and why Jesus chose not to come down off the cross to silence his mockers with a display of power. Ultimately, missional spirituality understands that Christ was subversive and disruptive to the hypocritical religious system. Missional spirituality incorporates the faith spoken of in Hebrews 11—those listed didn't see the promises given to them fulfilled, but they died with their eyes set on the prize, seeking to press on toward the upward call of Christ, to fight the good fight, to finish the race, and keep the faith, no matter what personal limitations or thorns in the flesh came their way.

DISCIPLESHIP TOOLS

Tools are the adaptable, practical methods that light our way. Like a handheld torch, tools illuminate specific areas of need or challenge, guiding our actions. Not every practice will be suitable for every situation. Therefore, careful discernment is crucial in selecting the right tool for the task. Once a particular tool effectively reveals solutions, we can apply it with increasing diligence and frequency, focusing our efforts where they are most needed.

Tool #1: CIM—Clarity, Intentionality, Methodology

To love God and seek first his kingdom we need to have a vision that is formed by God, a strong intention to push toward this vision faithfully, and the appropriate means to get there. This requires prayerful discernment.

In his classic book *Renovation of the Heart*, Dallas Willard identifies three key elements for any change: vision, intention, and means.[27] For our purposes, we will refer to these as clarity, intentionality, and methodology (CIM). There has been so much written on how to change, and in this information age we have all the information we need, yet we still see people failing to achieve the changes they aim for in their lives. We see people with seemingly great intentions but no follow-through. We see people with the appropriate means but lacking the willpower to pursue growth or change. We see people with the willpower and means but no vision for change, so change doesn't happen.

In CIM we find an irreducible minimum necessary for *true* and *lasting* transformation:

Clarity is the wise insight necessary to see the clear picture of what a preferred future can be; it is understanding what the end goal is and how to move patiently in that direction. Clarity is vital if we are to see any change in our lives, but it is only one part of the equation. We need *intentionality*—not mere desire but the deliberate inclination of all our willpower toward the right end. Intention is the actual application of effort toward the vision and goal. But with all the right intentions and vision, we will fail if we use the wrong methods! We need the appropriate and correct *methodology* to achieve the desired changes.

---

[27] Dallas Willard, *Renovation of the Heart: Putting on the Character of Christ* (NavPress, 2002).

Each of these areas requires a diligent, prayerful pursuit of truth. To discover the correct clarity, we must seek the Lord, pray, study, and invite others to speak into our lives. To strengthen intentionality, we must practice the spiritual practices revealed in Scripture (such as prayer, meditation on God's Word, solitude, fasting, fellowship, etc.) that enable growth in all parts of our being. To uncover the right methodology, we must be open and yielded to correction and ready to diligently search for the appropriate means. This takes hard work. But to the person who surrenders to the leading of the Holy Spirit in this journey, the fruit is rich and deep.

One of Willard's recurring mottos is instructive here: "Grace is not opposed to effort; it is opposed to earning." As we make disciples and practice the ways of Jesus, his grace is not opposed to our efforts in these areas. The grace of God works in accordance with those things to beget more grace. Grace is, however, opposed to anything we do with an "earning" mentality or a motivation to achieve our own value apart from him. In Ephesians 2, we are reminded that God is the first initiator. We were dead in our sins (something dead doesn't initiate anything!); but in Christ, he made us alive so that we can respond to his initiating grace and go on to do the good works that were prepared for us beforehand. Yet, we must not rely on our good works so that we are unable to boast about our achievements.

Willard's goal is to apply vision, intention, and means to discipleship. Our *clarity* of discipleship must be compelling. Too often Christians have a vision of discipleship that is just a bunch of rules and dead religion. Others view this idea of eternal life as the stereotypical cartoonish person sitting on a cloud with a harp. For many Christians, the collective vision of true union with the Triune God has been traded for counterfeit visions that just don't compel anyone to do anything valuable with their life, or they compel us to do things that seem valuable but don't have eternal or deep significance to who we are to be and who we are to become in God.

Our *intentionality* to be a follower of Christ must be diligent. We are commanded to live into the good works he has prepared for us in advance (Ephesians 2:10). We are invited to come into his presence.

Tool #2: "Gospel Fluency"[28]

When you are fluent in something, it should come so naturally that you don't even need to think about it. Fluency allows for instant flow and an intuitive expert response. Gospel fluency is when someone has allowed the good news of Jesus to permeate their mind, heart, and entire being so much so that they cannot help but slip naturally and frequently into good-news language. While many debate how to define the gospel, it is simple enough to use Paul's principle from Romans 1:16—the gospel is the power of God that results in salvation. We also know that the good news is that the kingdom of God is here and available for us to enter into.

These are all true aspects of how the Bible fleshes out this "good news." The good news has many sides to it and is, in one sense, infinitely deep and complex, yet the kernel of the gospel is a simple equation: Salvation and forgiveness and life are provided to us by God because of the work of Christ! At the same time, we must not insult the theological richness of the gospel by limiting it to such brief statements. A gospel-fluent understanding has been influenced by repeated reflection and application of the gospel to the deepest areas of our hearts, lives, and relationships. When the good news is applied so deeply and broadly to our lives, it will manifest itself in the culture we create around us. We will begin to overflow with his love, and his good news will spill out.

The point is: The good news of the kingdom of heaven is for you in every facet of your life. God offers complete wholeness, forgiveness, love, reconciliation, and freedom. It is by embracing this offer—this good news—that we can approach our entire lives—workplaces, relationships, circumstances—with the awareness that wholeness is a possibility and that hope is real. If you experience a broken relationship, the good news is that God is always offering hope for restoration. If you experience a loss, the good news is that Christ experienced the worst loss for your sake, and he extends his full life and eternal glorious

---

[28] "Gospel fluency" is a helpful term, but unfortunately it is sometimes used in a less-than-merciful sort of way. Therefore, we use the term cautiously here with the intention of clearly applying the good news to each area of life.

riches to you so that you can move from loss to fullness in him. The gospel applies to all situations.

Tool #3: The 4Gs

In *The Gospel Primer*, Caesar Kalinowski refers to the "4 Gs," which is a simple application of gospel fluency: God is Great, so I don't have to be in control; God is Glorious, so I don't have to fear others; God is Good, so I don't have to look elsewhere for my satisfaction; God is Gracious, so I don't have to prove myself.[29] The good news is that God is who we *need* him to be, not necessarily what our sinful hearts *want* him to be; but he will always be exactly what is needed. The learning curve is for us to align with who he is and embrace his sufficiency in every aspect of our lives. His life then becomes my life, so "it is no longer I who live, but Christ who lives in me" (Galatians 2:20). Union with Christ can become the constant, powerful reality in which we live.

Tool #4: SEARCH

As we study the life of Christ and the values and priorities he demonstrated (which the early church followed after his ascension), *and* as we take into consideration the *whole counsel* of the Word of God, we see certain patterns that are beneficial in learning to walk with the Lord. The vision is growing in him and honoring him with all areas of our lives surrendered to him. Slow movement in the right direction for a long period of time makes a great difference!

SEARCH is an acronym for a daily set of questions that enables us to regularly consider how we may yield to Jesus as Lord in each area of our lives in a grace-based, *non*-religious manner.[30]

---

[29] Kalinowski, *The Gospel Primer*, 99.

[30] This tool was inspired by Michael Frost's "BELLS" from his book *Surprise the World*, which we would highly recommend. Michael Frost, *Surprise the World: The Five Habits of Highly Missional People* (NavPress, 2015).

- **Savior:** How am I seeing Christ as Savior today?
- **Engage:** Who can I engage with the good news and with love?
- **Act of love:** What small act of love can I intentionally stretch myself to do for a neighbor or associate?
- **Rest:** How am I letting Jesus lead me to still waters and green pastures? How am I letting him restore my soul (c.f. Psalm 23)?
- **Confess:** How is the Lord calling me to humility? Is there anything I need to confess to him and to close spiritual friends?
- **Home:** How is my home life? Am I keeping enough margin to react in healthy ways to emergencies and the needs of those I am committed to?

Tool #5: In, Out, Up

In chapter five on organic systems, we will unpack In, Out, Up in detail as a means of organic discipleship. The basic concept is that every community and individual needs to be attentive to the work of the Lord in their life:

- **In:** how God is shaping you
- **Out:** how he is calling you into his mission
- **Up:** worship

This is a holistic approach to discipleship that allows for robust transformation.

Tool #6: Head, Heart, Hands

This tool helps us to be comprehensive and holistic in our approach to spiritual growth. If we focus only on one or two of these three elements, our lives will be imbalanced. But, if we engage all three, we will see holistic and complementary growth that deeply enriches our lives.

- **Head:** To fill our minds with God's truth through study— engaging with theological and spiritual books, listening to sermons, meditating on the Word, and exploring missional practices and methodology in order to faithfully contextualize the gospel within our culture.

- **Hands:** To enact gospel truth through practical expression—moving from theory to action (just as Jesus led his disciples to practice what he taught them), learning to use our gifts in our community, and tangibly loving our neighbors.
- **Heart:** To nurture our inner being—cultivating our character, integrity, emotional well-being, and deeper intimacy with Christ by feeding on him as our soul's refuge and strength, and learning his unforced rhythms of grace (Matthew 11:28–30 MSG).[31]

Mature discipleship is *not* about action for the sake of action; it is *not* about knowledge for the sake of knowledge; it *is* about the integrity of character and godliness that is developed during the maturing process of becoming a Christlike servant. Jesus wants our hearts more than anything else!

Tool #7: What, How, Who?

This tool includes three questions to ask when we engage the Scriptures in study.[32]

- **What?** When we come to Scripture, we always need to ask the "what" question: What is it saying? What does it mean? What is the Lord highlighting to my heart in this passage? This is the observation *and* the interpretation element, but it is also the

---

[31] An excellent book on the heart is Crawford W. Loritts' *Leadership as an Identity: The Four Traits of Those Who Wield Lasting Influence* (Moody, 2009), in which he identifies what it looks like to have a heart of integrity rather than just fancy "hand" skills and "head" knowledge. Loritts is the real deal. This book is absolutely one of the best books we have ever read. Jeremy took a class with Loritts years ago, and Loritts had fifty people praying in a room a thousand miles away during every minute the class was in session. Needless to say, Jeremy left class each day and took a prayer walk to repent and to process what the Lord was depositing in his heart.

[32] We recommend other acronyms for study too but won't develop them here ("SOAP"—Scripture, Observation, Application, Prayer; and "OIA"—Observation, Interpretation, Application).

personal, relational question of what the Lord wants to do in our lives. What is he saying to me now? Answering this question leads to an obedience-oriented response.

- **How?** This question focuses on application and obedience. It must always be asked with grace! This step must not become legalism; it is a gracious cooperation with the Spirit's leading in our lives: How am I going to respond to his Word? How am I going to obey this? How am I going to change? How am I going to practice this revealed truth?

- **Who?** Too often Bible studies become just that—Bible studies—not leading to a transformed life or an awareness of others, but merely for the purpose of making us feel good about our knowledge and insight into the Word. We have become very good at talking about obedience without truly following Jesus. Bible studies can easily create a self-deceptive culture as we become hearers merely deceiving ourselves and not doers of the Word (James 1:22). To avoid this, we must ask ourselves: Who is the Lord putting on my heart to serve as a result of this truth in his Word?

Jeremy once led a microchurch through these questions and was shocked to see the results. There were a few guys in the group who had been in church their entire lives who could *always* give immediate answers to the "what" question. They were also good at talking about the "how" question, although they found it much harder. However, it took over a month before they were finally able to understand what the "who" question really meant. Each week they would say, "My 'who' for the week is me." They couldn't take their eyes off themselves. They couldn't think of anyone in their lives they could serve or minister to. Jeremy would keep saying, "The 'who' is about who you will serve, sacrifice for, or minister to."

When the group finally began to click this, one guy said, "This week, my 'who' is my friend at work who has been struggling." Another said, "This week, my 'who' is my mom who is very sick right now. I can go above and beyond to take care of her!" The joy that these guys suddenly started experiencing in their lives was unbelievable. They were becoming conduits of God's love for others. Jeremy praised the Lord as he witnessed God's Holy Spirit *graciously* convicting them.

Tool #8: Components of Comprehensive Discipleship

There are many areas of discipleship that we tend to overlook in our churches and discipleship programs. Ken Boa gives us a list of "biblical views" that reminds us of areas that are sometimes neglected when thinking about discipleship.[33] Take some time to review this list and think of those you are currently ministering to. Are there areas that you can use to help take them *beyond* their current understanding of discipleship and into new growth?

- Biblical views of the authority and truth of Scripture, our value system, hope, purpose, motivations, contentment and gratitude, work and leisure
- The development of personal convictions
- The transformative role of trials in our lives
- The challenges our culture presents to a Christian understanding of the kingdom
- The nature of spiritual warfare and the resources the Holy Spirit makes available to us
- The process of spiritual formation

IT'S SCRIPTURAL. IT'S RATIONAL. IT'S TRANSFORMATIONAL.

When we examine disciple-making in Jesus' context of first-century Palestine, and his followers' methods in the New Testament, we see that disciple-making is intrinsically relational, Christ-oriented, love-permeated, grace-based, truth-infused, and multiplication-oriented. The tools mentioned in this chapter can help you in this journey. We

---

[33] Kenneth Boa, *Conformed to His Image: Biblical and Practical Approaches to Spiritual Formation* (Zondervan, 2001), 379.

highly encourage you to study discipleship by reading the Gospels of Matthew, Luke, and John; and observe these things for yourself.

In addition to being biblical, what we have presented is rational. If you are going to make an apprentice who passes on the desired DNA to someone else with a multiplication mentality, then these principles will facilitate successful reproduction.

Not only do these disciple-making principles and tools "work" in the sense of multiplication, but they are also transformational. We have seen all of these principles tested and demonstrated to be fruitful. At the time of writing, we have both been blessed to see the fruits of multiplication from over thirty years of ministry. Some we discipled many years ago have multiplied by discipling others who have discipled others. We are "great-grandparents" in our disciple-making efforts, for we have seen our spiritual sons and daughters bear spiritual sons and daughters who continued to bear fruit to the third and even fourth generations. This testifies to the power of Jesus' principles at work. These principles and practices are transformational! Each has been tested and demonstrated to be fruitful and effective.

3

INCARNATIONAL LIVING
Adopting a Missional Strategic Mindset

 KEY IDEAS

- The gospel is for you! Slow down, take a deep breath, and let God's grace motivate you. Any changes needed in your life are best conducted with a posture of learning and practicing—not "trying" but "training," not "straining" but "strengthening." The good news is that Jesus frees us to keep moving from glory to glory, from one level of maturity to another.
- While "incarnation" literally means to *be in the flesh* or to *embody*, for our context here, "incarnational" describes *being with*—to be among and to be *for* the people you are loving. This one paradigm can change everything in terms of how you relate to people. Imitating Christ by living among and for the people around you can be powerfully transformative, both for you and for those around you.
- We need to understand the original meaning of the word "evangelism" as the spreading of overwhelmingly good news to others.

- There are a variety of approaches to evangelism. This chapter releases you to engage with evangelism as the Lord has intended for *you*—to discover what works best with who he has made you to be and who he is equipping you to reach.
- We must approach our relationship with the world around us in wisdom (Colossians 4:5), having a listening and learning posture, with respect to the person, the context, and the culture around us. Having considered these elements, we can discern the most effective method of communicating God's unchanging truth of love as good news to each individual. Given this is highly complex, we must approach this with wisdom and maturity. This chapter contains simple tools to help you along the way.

SEE FOR YOURSELF

Read the books of Luke, John, or Acts and ask yourself: What do these books show me about how Jesus was on mission? What did mission look like for the early church? How can my mission today align with these examples?

To go further, read through all the writings of Paul. Ask yourself: What mindset and perspective did Paul seem to maintain? What was driving him?

INCARNATIONAL LIVING FOUNDATIONS

Foundations are our unshakable core map, charting the terrain. Foundations provide the rock-solid theological principles that remain constant, regardless of the specific location or context we find ourselves in. They equip and prepare us for the journey, ensuring we have a reliable understanding of the fundamental landscape.

Foundation #1: Living the Good News

Jesus said he only participated in doing what the Father was doing (John 5:19). Jesus became flesh, incarnating himself in this world. In a similar way, we are to embody the practices of Jesus—we "go and be" among the people.

Hugh Halter and Matt Smay, authors of *The Tangible Kingdom Primer*, note,

> You might have noticed ... people don't like to be "evangelized." They don't automatically think our truths are their truths. They won't show up at our church gatherings to hear our ideas and they can't stand it when we push them to accept our concepts.[1]

Conversely, they observe how effective it is to love, show hope, share good news, and do good deeds. More often than not, people receive acts of kindness and listen to good news that truly strikes them as *good news*—they want to hear something good and encouraging. People allow us into their lives when they see that our actions are consistent with what they perceive as true kindness—when it is sincere and without additional agendas or manipulation.

However, Scripture also includes a host of role models who didn't always just "say what people wanted to hear." They were people of confidence and courage who knew that sometimes truth needs to be communicated in ways that may be difficult for others to acknowledge. When we take our cues from Jesus, we find that he dealt with this tension perfectly! We have our best role model in Christ, who knew when to speak, how to speak, and what to speak (and when *not* to speak). Jesus brought light, life, truth, grace, and love. His Spirit will guide us, and where he guides, the presence of the Spirit's fruit is a confirmation to us that we are headed in the right direction. When we listen to his Spirit and follow his ways, living incarnationally becomes increasingly clear and compelling as a way of life.

---

[1] Hugh Halter and Matt Smay, *The Tangible Kingdom Primer: An Eight-Week Guide to Incarnational Community* (Missio Publishing, 2009), ix.

Foundation #2: A Missionary God

God created this world, and all that is in it. Adam sinned and brought the cursed realities of sin into our world. God immediately promised to send a savior (the ultimate missionary) to bring salvation and ultimately restoration to the *entire universe*. Jesus is a missionary; the Father is the ultimate sender of the ultimate missionary; and the Holy Spirit is the missionary sent to dwell in us, who leads us to operate as a family of missionary servants. Missiology (the cause of God) is the appropriate context for our ecclesiology (our understanding of church).[2]

Foundation #3: Mission Flows from Identity

The word "missional" has often been overused and abused, so let's define it here: To be truly missional is to be in full alignment with God's agenda for the expansion of his kingdom in this world. Being missional *must* flow from our identity of who we are rather than be an activity that we do. When we use this word, it pertains to a direction or orientation of our actions and lives as those sent forth as missionary people from a missionary God.

The history of missions reminds us that sometimes believers cross the globe for the purpose of being who we are called to be (a people sent forth). Yet, in 1 Peter 2:9, we read, "But you are a chosen race, a royal priesthood, a holy nation, a people for his own possession, that you may proclaim the excellencies of him who called you out of darkness into his marvelous light." Peter reminds us we are a "chosen spiritual race of people" (our own theologically expanded paraphrase). We are a class or an order of bearers of the divine image, and as such, we are a royal priesthood. This means that we are a people ordained by a King, who has put his kingly stamp and identity upon us! We are a kingly people, and we are simultaneously a kingly priesthood. A

---

[2] An excellent read on this topic is David Bosch, *Transforming Mission: Paradigm Shifts in Theology of Mission* (Orbis Books, 1991).

priesthood is a collection of people whose purpose is to intercede, to point people to God, and to help connect people to the Triune God. As a kingly priesthood, we are also a holy nation. Our allegiance is pledged to no flag before Christ. Our true national identity is eternal, royal, and spiritual. We are citizens of heaven. We have been made a people for his own possession *so that* we may proclaim his excellencies! He saved us, shaped us, and made us part of his household so that we can participate in the good works that he has prepared for us to participate in. He has called us out of darkness into his glorious, incredible, mind-blowing light. He has taken us who were dead and made us fully alive in Christ Jesus.

Our King has determined our identity and sent us forth. Jesus said that as the Father sent him, so also, he sends us into this world (John 20:21).

Our identity as a people is as a family of servants who are sent into this world. This is what it means to be missional. We have the mission of God within us, and we walk in accordance with his heartbeat of love. A growing number of sources now describe missional community as, "A family of missionary servants sent to serve the world and make disciples of Jesus." This idea—"family of missionary servants"—has struck a chord with communities of faith seeking to be Jesus-followers.

Foundation #4: Walking in Step with the Spirit

We can only communicate the love of Jesus when our mission flows from a posture of love and humility founded in our identity in Christ.

Understanding our identity in Christ allows us to see his mission all around us, as we follow his leading and walk in the power of his Holy Spirit. This great news of life in Christ wells up inside of us and spills out.

Imitating Jesus will lead us toward missional living, incarnational living, and evangelism as a product of our identity (not just a product of our activity). As a product of our identity and maturity as followers of Jesus, we love people in the ways that they need to be loved and communicate with them in ways that are inspired by the Holy Spirit's promptings. We also learn how to remain silent, to intercede through prayer, solitude, and self-control.

Often, evangelism happens best when God shows us what he is already doing with the person in front of us. We have a greater awareness of God's love for that person and what he is wanting to work in their life. This is where being open to the Holy Spirit's leading and knowing the Holy Spirit leading and empowering you is vital. Missional living, then, can involve speaking particular words or taking particular action, as you are led by God; but many times it also involves a *lack* of action, or restraining from speaking or action, as you trust in God's divine work and timing.

Foundation #5: God's Sovereignty and Our Responsibility

Throughout Scripture, our missionary God emphasizes his sovereignty over salvation, while also framing human responsibility and responsiveness to his actions. It is clear that God works in us and we also respond to his working. There is a tension here that is beautiful and mysterious. Debates about this tension can cause distraction that leads people away from loving God and people and toward confident assertions about theological positions, prowess, knowledge, and superiority. (Paul has a lot to say about these sorts of people in his letters to Timothy and Titus.)

The secret workings of that tension belong to God, but what has been revealed is for us (Deuteronomy 29:29).

In his classic book *Evangelism and the Sovereignty of God*, J. I. Packer concludes that it is God's power that gives us hope in sharing his message with others because we know that his message can be effective.[3] We can trust the fruit to the Lord. This releases us from taking responsibility upon ourselves for that which only the Spirit can accomplish. It also puts our hearts in a place of humility as we trust him to do his work. As Jesus said in Mark 4, the kingdom of heaven is like a farmer who scatters seed, goes to sleep, then wakes up and the

---

[3]   J. I. Packer, *Evangelism and the Sovereignty of God* (InterVarsity Press, 2012).

seed has grown; but the farmer does not know all of the dynamics as to why or how the seed has grown. The farmer just plants the seed and entrusts the rest of the process to the Lord.

We shouldn't allow God's sovereignty in salvation to prevent us from interacting in an intentional way with others who have not yet trusted in Christ; we should scatter the seed. Likewise, we shouldn't allow the idea of human responsibility to cause us to see God as impotent or to become guilt-ridden under unbearable yokes that we cannot possibly carry, thinking that we alone are responsible for the supernatural work that only the Holy Spirit can do.

Foundation #6: Exploring the Incarnational

If incarnation is about becoming an embodied representation of God's good news among others, it cannot be seen as separate from mission. Halter and Smay say that incarnational is the "inseparable twin" of missional.

> If missional means "to go," incarnation is about how you go and what people see as you go. It encompasses your posture, your tone, your motives, and your heart. Incarnation is critical because it will eventually determine whether or not people will want to know you or your God.[4]

As *The Message* version says, "The Word became flesh and blood and moved into the neighborhood" (John 1:14 MSG). Think about how Jesus dealt with the woman accused of adultery. The Law claimed that she would have to be stoned to death, yet when the spiritual leaders of the day brought her before Jesus, he said, "Let him who is without sin among you be the first to throw a stone at her" (John 8:7). Christ led them to examine their own hearts, with each of them concluding they couldn't claim such piety. By doing this, Jesus put the woman's sin within the universal context of human sinfulness. As author Debra

---

4   Halter and Smay, *The Tangible Kingdom Primer*, 26.

Hirsch likes to say, "Jesus leveled the playing field!" He put us all on the same page. Jesus then asked the woman where her accusers were (v. 10) and she replied that they had all gone away. He then said, "Neither do I condemn you; go, and from now on sin no more" (v. 11).

Jesus' posture was one of love. But notice that he also commanded her to do something that she was incapable of doing: going and never sinning again. He sent her on her way, but only after planting the seed that would require her to *always depend on Christ* for her salvation.

Beautiful. Jesus was such a genius! In his brilliant love, he allowed her to be saved from punishment, removed condemnation from her, then planted the seed that would require her to find him as Savior. But why didn't he also say in that moment, "I am the Way, the Truth and the Life; you can't get to the Father except through me"? Why didn't he say, "Now, pray this prayer with me and put your faith in me..."? Instead, he sent her on her way and planted the seed of love, the seed that would cause her to search. Jesus knew that the Holy Spirit was working in this woman's heart. Jesus saw what the Father was doing and lovingly participated. We would do well to take notes on incarnational evangelism from this story, as it exemplifies the posture we need to adopt today. A common experience some people have with their missional communities or churches is the sense that, "I can't bring my friends here." They intuitively know that their friends will feel judged, hated, uneasy, uncomfortable, as if they don't belong, or as cultural outcasts in Christendom. But if a community of Jesus-followers can practice the posture of incarnation, then we will be capable of loving any individual in the way the Holy Spirit leads us to.

In his book *Abba's Child*, Brennan Manning mentions an encounter with a young lady who was a cult member.[5] Brennan and his friend were eating ice-cream, when a young woman tried to "push" her cult ideologies on them. His initial inclination was that this was a repugnant activity and that she, as a cult member, was naive and duped by a well-known, dangerous cult leader. Brennan's first impulse was to be repelled by her. But instead, he told her that he admired

---

[5] Brennan Manning, *Abba's Child: The Cry of the Heart for Intimate Belonging* (NavPress, 2015).

the fact that she was living in accordance with her deeply held beliefs. Instead of pointing out how wrong she was and that she needed to repent, he followed Jesus' way of communicating that "neither do I condemn you." Immediately, the girl looked at him and asked, "Are you a Christian?" He affirmed that he was, and she began weeping, saying that all week, Christians had been angry with her, yelling at her, and that one Christian woman had even physically hit her with a Bible! Brennan was the first Christian who had looked at her and treated her with real love. That woman understood what real love was, and she surely hadn't seen it in the religious order of Christianity until Brennan incarnated love by bringing her an encouragement. Have we sometimes pushed people away from even wanting to hear the message of Jesus because we were so determined to point out how they were wrong?

Foundation #7: Evangelism Clarified

The term "evangelism," although often used in contemporary Christianity, isn't found directly in Scripture (or its Greek equivalent). Instead, the Bible frequently uses the term "gospel" (meaning "good news") and explicitly mentions the role of the "evangelist"—both in its original Greek and through the examples of people in the text. This distinction is important, especially considering how the term "evangelism" is sometimes misused.

Evangelism or evangelizing, then, is actually a derivative implied by the sheer existence of "good news" combined with the actions of people who communicate the good news. If we see evangelism as the implication of the biblical language (good news and the evangelist who shares the good news), then we have the clarity needed to unpack how we can be carriers of good news in our time. Biblically speaking, "evangel" (good news) is a noun. The modern derivative verb is the action of speaking forth the good news that there is salvation in Jesus. As a noun, it is the gift of grace that is given by the power of the Holy Spirit to enable people to speak forth that message. But as a gift of grace from the Holy Spirit, we cannot possibly do true evangelism in our own power, worked up by our own sheer volition. Since evangelism is a product of the indwelling presence of the Holy Spirit, then it must logically, by all forms of reason and rationality, be something that *he* works through us as we yield to his power. So, all books with method-ologies (including *this* book) must never allow us to learn to trust our intellect over the leading and guidance of the Holy Spirit of God Almighty. True teaching about evangelism begins with helping people to listen to the Holy Spirit, to discern what the Spirit of the Father is doing, and then to act according to his guidance.

Ken Boa mentions a number of principles that formulate a philosophy of evangelism.[6] We have found these principles to be freeing and powerful in helping us keep perspective when it comes to this area of our lives and ministry.

- **Evangelism is an ongoing work.** (See the parables of Jesus indicating organic stages of growth in Mark 4.) People's hearts move in one of two directions—toward Christ or away from him. It is sufficient to say that on one end of the spectrum, a person may have hatred toward Christ and the gospel, but over time, they may become open, then begin to have faith, then begin responding more to grace and growing more in that faith, and eventually move toward reproducing his love in others around them. Evangelism includes preparing the soil, planting the gospel seed in the soil, cultivating the soil, and reaping a harvest.

  This also aligns with Don Everts and Doug Schaupp's conclusions in *I Once Was Lost.*[7] Their research project studied thousands of people who had formerly been skeptics and recently committed their lives to follow Jesus. They noticed some patterns in how people moved toward Christ. A person might be initially skeptical, but then begins to trust someone who follows Jesus. Next, they begin to be curious about how that Jesus-follower lives their life, and they become open to change in their own life (any

---

[6] Boa, *Conformed to His Image*, chapter 32.

[7] Don Everts and Doug Schaupp, *I Once Was Lost: What Postmodern Skeptics Taught Us About Their Path to Jesus* (InterVarsity Press, 2008).

type of change). This person suddenly finds themselves in a place of being willing to consider new ideas and new approaches to life. They then begin to believe in the existence of some sort of god (not necessarily Jesus), until finally they put their faith in Christ.

Awareness of this process can give us joy, hope, and patience as we love those around us. Recognizing that each person is at a different place on their own spiritual journey, we can patiently let the Lord do the work. As Boa says, "The key concept to be gleaned from this process principle is the liberating truth that if we are involved in any one of these ... phases, we are doing evangelism."[8]

- **The outcome is in God's hands.** This is beautiful and so good to know. How freeing! Plant the seed, then go rest. He will do the supernatural work.

- **Planting seeds and tending the soil takes more time and energy than harvesting.** The person concerned with *reaping* will tend to focus on the end result, proclamation, immediate results, individual effort, points of disagreement, answers, justice, and courage. The person concerned with *sowing* will tend to focus on preparing the way, gentle persuasion, gradual change, team impact, common ground, questions, love, and wisdom. This isn't to say that one is better than the other, but each must discover how to walk within these tensions in a way that honors the Lord. Only focusing on one side of this coin—sowing or reaping—can create an imbalance.

- **Evangelism has eternal effects.** Evangelism is a way of being rich toward God, seeking first his eternal kingdom, and following him ("Follow me, and I will send you out to fish for people" Matthew 4:19 NIV). We are to view people as his image-bearers, each one bearing a soul with an eternal destiny and the eternal image of God.

---

[8] Boa, *Conformed to His Image*, 392.

- **Evangelism can have the wrong motivations.** Guilt, pride, fear of not "appeasing" an overtly religious authoritarian impression of God, etc., are not appropriate motivation.
- **Evangelism involves both the message and the messenger.** It's both show and tell.
- **True evangelism is integrated within discipleship.** As indicated earlier, evangelism is a subset of discipleship. The goal in gospel conversations is to help people see Jesus (who he is and what he accomplished by his death and resurrection), and to become followers of him, not just to have some spiritual or emotive experience that quickly washes away or is choked out by thorns (Mark 4).

Foundation #8: Evangelism is *Not* ...

Boa gives a few examples of what evangelism is *not* and misconceptions that we should be aware of. Evangelism is *not*:

- **Notches on the belt**—looking for notches on your belt to add to your list of "effective influence" in order to build yourself up by attaching your identity to achievements.
- **Transactional**—forcing a reductionistic message about Jesus into every conversation to assuage our guilt that any relationships we have aren't justified until we have evangelized the other person. This understanding has prevented many Christians from even knowing how to have real friendships. We make every relationship transactionally oriented to the point that we have forgotten how to just be friends for the sake of being friends and how to love for the sake of love.
- **Deceptive**—the bait-and-switch mentality has often reversed the intended effects of evangelism. Think about the awkwardness of some multilevel marketing groups that make you think a meeting is about one thing, only to have you sit for a couple hours while they sell you a product or recruit you to sell their products. Ugh!

- **Forceful**—evangelism is not a way of shoving truth down people's throats.[9]

Foundation #9: Disciplism

In his book *Disciplism*, Alan Hirsch points out that as we focus on making disciples, evangelism happens even more because we are showing people how to follow Jesus.[10] The gospel begins with the simplest truth: Jesus invites us to put our confidence in him and begin following him right now into his eternal kingdom.[11]

As we have personally practiced these truths, we have seen a new understanding develop: pre-conversion discipleship. It may sound offensive to some and funny to others, but we started using this term because we realized that many of our friends were beginning to become "followers" or "disciples" of Jesus, even though they wouldn't have called themselves "Christians" yet. Then we began hearing of people worldwide who were seeing this same phenomenon! Pre-conversion discipleship means we help people begin to take steps toward confidence in Christ and practicing the things that constitute his kingdom. By following Jesus, even the worst of sinners can begin a new way of living (John 14:6).

Foundation #10: Motivations

Without love, nothing we do makes sense. Without love, nothing is truly right or appropriate or effective. The beginning of our love is to know the love of God that comes to us through Christ, through his Spirit, through creation, through his good gifts, through his common grace, and his general revealing of himself to us. We love because *he first loved us* (1 John 4:19). The only basis for this sort of love comes

---

[9] Boa, *Conformed to His Image*, 399.

[10] Hirsch, *Disciplism*.

[11] See Matthew 4:17, Mark 1:15, and Luke 10:9. Jesus declared directly and commanded his disciples to declare directly that the kingdom of heaven is near and available.

from a transformed understanding of and experience with the love of God. We respond to God in love, loving him, loving his values, and loving his ways. This leads us to love our neighbors, friends, enemies, and all people out of the overflow of God's love for us.

When we begin to love others because they bear God's image, ministry to them flows supernaturally through us. We also love them out of self-forgetfulness—it isn't about us; it's about loving them.[12] If we are not self-forgetful, we can end up loving people only to create unhealthy codependences: We somehow "love" them in order to feed our own savior complex or our own self-worth by achieving some spiritual goal. But if we remove ourselves from the picture and walk in our identity, then we become the love of God toward others.

As Boa points out, motivations for living an incarnational life include:

- **Gratitude**—thankfulness that the Lord has done so much good in our lives, causing us to want others to experience his goodness too. We are also grateful for the other person's existence, so we want to participate in adding goodness to them.
- **Spiritual reward**—When we serve others, we are rewarded with the deepening realities of the fruit of God's presence—the fruit of the Spirit and all the good things that Christ passes on to us—and we are also helping others experience those same realities. This is a biblical motivation for serving others.
- **Identity**—as we walk in our identity in Christ, we cannot help but serve and love others in an incarnational way.
- **Purpose**—we find immense purpose in loving others as described above. It affirms the deep nature of what we are called to do as a royal priesthood, *and* we also want to help others discover their purpose in life.
- **Hope**—we have an eternally deep awareness of God. Eternity is written on our hearts; we feel him; we know him; and knowing

---

[12] See Timothy Keller's short book *The Freedom of Self-Forgetfulness: The Path to True Christian Joy* (10Publishing, 2012).

him is eternal life itself (John 17:3). So out of this determined hope, we cannot help but plant seeds of hope all around us. Because we are so deeply convinced of this being our true reality, it happens naturally.

- **A longing for God**—longing for more of him; longing to experience every good thing we have in him through the sharing of our faith with others (Philemon 6); longing for others to experience his goodness.[13]

Foundation #11: Invisible Ministry

Never lose heart! We won't always see immediate results for faithfulness, but in every area of life, we must learn to *not* be motivated by immediate results. It would be unrealistic for a counselor to expect his clients to be "fixed" after their first meeting, or for a doctor to expect her patients to be cured after one recommendation. So why do we typically focus on immediate results in our evangelistic circles and practices in the church?

Alan Hirsch suggests we can get caught up in a "Road to Damascus" lens that clouds our understanding: We imagine light shining down from heaven upon someone every time we share the gospel (as Saul experienced his conversion in Acts 9). If the light doesn't shine and miracles don't happen, we think something went wrong. We often forget the "Road to Emmaus" narrative (Luke 24), which frees us from this way of thinking. The disciples walked with Jesus himself on the road to Emmaus, and they didn't even know it! It wasn't until they broke bread with him that their eyes were opened, and they realized that he had been speaking to them about *himself* the entire time.

Release your expectation of instant results. Jesus gave us a better way. We have freedom in the ways of the King and his kingdom. When we plant seeds, we know that they will land on various soils. Some will land on hardened soil and will not grow; others will seem to grow, only to be crowded out by weeds or scorched by the sun; and

---

[13] Boa, *Conformed to his Image*, chapters 11–12.

others will grow and multiply (Matthew 13:3–8). But we just do the work of planting as he calls us. Fruit may remain invisible for a long time. Many of the most influential people in the history of Christianity didn't see effective results in their ministry for years and sometimes even decades. Yet they remained faithful to sowing seeds.

Many of the heroes of the faith who are mentioned in Hebrews 11 never saw the fulfilment of the promises God had given them. Patience is essential. No one plants a seed and expects an orchard the next day!

There was a janitor in Jeremy's elementary school who knew every student by name, even though he only connected with a small number of them during his time working there. A teacher said that "Jim" prayed for every single one of the students by name. The prayers of that janitor, a humble servant, may have been more instrumental than most people can imagine. The fruit is often invisible unless you see with eyes trained on the kingdom of heaven.

INCARNATIONAL LIVING PARADIGMS

Paradigms are our guiding compass for contextual insight. Paradigms offer a solid framework, acting like a compass that orients us within our context, showing the possible directions we can travel. They shape how we see and interpret our surroundings, guiding the complex work of application.

Paradigm #1: Christ and Culture

What people mean when they talk about mission, incarnation, and evangelism will be greatly influenced by their broader philosophy of ministry, Christ, and culture. This has historically been subject to great debate. Alan Roxburgh, in his work *Missional*, provides an insightful illustration of this, which we have recreated below in our own words:[14]

Imagine three friends who once had an excellent and intimate friendship, but life slowly took them across the planet and out of each other's lives for a long period of time. Over the years, they would plan

---

[14] Alan J. Roxburgh, *Missional: Joining God in the Neighborhood* (Baker, 2011).

to reconnect and, when they got together, it would be as if no time had passed. Their friendship stayed intact and strong; they were on the same page. But as the years passed, a particularly long stretch of time kept them apart. Finally, one friend invited the other two over for a week. This friend offered to pay all the costs and to provide the schedule and everything needed. The other friends were overjoyed at this opportunity! When the three of them got together, the friend who was hosting talked only about himself for the entire first day. Initially, this was a bit frustrating, but the other friends, patient and understanding, figured he just needed to get some things off his chest. But day after day, to their grief, the host friend only spoke of himself, everything he had been doing, and everything he planned on doing. Whenever the others tried to speak, he interrupted them and returned all the focus to himself, his values, his methods, and his perspectives.

The host friend in this parable is the church. The church has become so self-focused that it always talks about itself and what it is doing, never really giving room for the culture or Christ to speak. Now, let's use this parable to help us with discernment regarding the church (and not for condemnation). While some churches offer a listening ear to those around them, too often we, as the church, have been so obsessed with how we create our own insider culture that we have refused to listen to the culture outside the church or be attentive to people around us, thinking that we have all the answers. Likewise, we have often become so rationally minded in our theological and ecclesiological systems that we have spoken over the voice of the Holy Spirit. We have become quite professional in our use of good programs with good intentions and established a good internal culture, yet sometimes at the cost of quenching the Spirit of God and the voices of those who are hurting around us.

How you understand *culture* is vital. How you understand the role of culture in the church is vital. How you understand the church and the role of Christ in the church and in the culture will together play out in how you live and do mission. Culture is made up of the perceptions, values, and actions of a people group. Culture is observed by people, internalized, then digested, only to reemerge in the reflexive actions of the observers (externalization). The effect of externalization is the formation of new culture which makes it "a thing" (turning values into realities). It is then observed again and reinternalized, repeating this process.

Historically, the church has debated how to approach *culture*. Timothy Keller suggests that the way forward is to create "a careful balance among several polarities." Keller addresses Richard Niebuhr's well-known polarities, which include:

- **Christ *against* culture**—we withdraw from the external culture into the church culture instead.
- **Christ *of* culture**—we accommodate God's work within the culture and look to affirm it; this focus is on being relevant to the culture.
- **Christ *above* culture**—we build upon and supplement the good within the culture, ultimately aiming to create synthesis above and beyond the culture, yet with the culture.
- **Christ and culture *in paradox***—this view is dualistic; we see one realm of sacred and one realm of secular. This leads to a paradigm that aims to strongly challenge the surrounding culture as our enemy.
- **Christ *transforming* culture**—we aim to transform and convert every part of culture into a new Christ-altered culture.[15]

Keller goes on to say that all five of these models are both right *and* wrong. Any one of them could easily become a one-size fits all rule and promote legalism, which could create incredible trouble and unnecessary pain. Taking any model to that extreme would actually remove the need for maturity, wisdom, and discernment. Maturity, wisdom, and discernment enable us to make good use of the strengths of each model: Do any of these models make sense as the logical and Spirit-led reaction to the culture? Is it possible that each of these models has

---

[15] For more on this, see Keller, *Center Church* chapters 16–17. Keller's approach is the most excellent example of engaging Christ and culture that we have come across.

its appointed time and season as the appropriate response to various elements of the surrounding culture?

How you understand these polarities will bear greatly on your incarnational style and evangelism. Some Christians approach evangelism as the good news on display through our actions of justice and systemic change in this world; some see the need to tear down strongholds of evil in the culture; some see the beauty of people who bear the image of God, and therefore they see the culture as being loaded with nuances of the image of God, in desperate need of affirmation and partnership; some see evangelism as directly speaking the good news into a person's life; and still others will see it as a complex dedication to cultivating the image of God in another person, aiming to nurture them toward his truth and away from falsehood and pain. Unfortunately, too many Christians part ways when they find themselves disagreeing on these issues. In reality we need each other's insights and partnership for maximum impact and the highest glory of the Lord in this world. No matter how you approach these topics, start with the appropriate motivations and foundations.

Paradigm #2: Love as *Real* Love

The missiologist and missional practitioner, Duane Elmer once spoke to me (Jeremy) of Western missionaries in Africa who thought they were serving the local leaders by telling them what "worked" back home. The local leaders did not see this as true servanthood, as they believed true servanthood is about asking questions instead of giving answers. Once the missionaries learned this, they began asking the local leaders questions. Their relationship grew stronger from that point forward because the local leaders felt truly loved and respected. This works the same way in our lives. Are we living incarnationally in a way that makes sense only to us? Are we doing evangelism in a way that makes sense only to us? Or, are we learning the maturity that goes beyond a one-size-fits-all approach—practicing his presence and allowing his Holy Spirit to guide us as we discern how to live in his kingdom?

Sometimes we need to stop and ask others how they need to be served, what their perceived needs are, and what they think we can do to help. At other times, it may be obvious how we need to love someone in a given moment. Let us cultivate the deep humility that loves people in ways that open the door for the gospel to transform their lives, rather than assuming that we can blow the door open with a few common approaches that work best for us. Learning to follow Jesus will require all of us to humbly reshape our relational intelligence.

Paradigm #3: A Conversation *Already Happening*

The Spirit of God is working in the hearts of all people. He has put his image in them, so he appeals to the eternity written in their souls. He pours out common grace that is both prevenient (working upon their souls, wooing them, calling to them) and effective (it bears results and doesn't return void). He gives general revelation to all through his eternal deity and power on display in all creation, as Paul speaks of in Romans 1 and as is referenced in many of the Psalms. On top of all this, he incarnated himself into human flesh to demonstrate how much he loves us and that by the gracious power of his Holy Spirit, we become capable of moving toward full redemption, restoration, and goodness.

Because of these realities, there is always a conversation already happening between God and any person we meet. The person may not know it, or they may be intentionally trying to quench/silence it, but that doesn't change the fact that God is still speaking to them in innumerable ways. Eugene Peterson refers to this fact throughout *The Contemplative Pastor*, where he reminds us that whenever we talk to someone, we must not barge into the middle of what the Lord is already saying/doing there.[16] Rather, we come in with contemplative patience; we meet an individual; we consider what the Father is doing; then we participate.

Only do what you see the Father doing. Wait on the Lord. Don't assume that you know exactly what a person needs, but wait for the

---

[16] Peterson, *The Contemplative Pastor*.

Lord to make things clear. Pray, asking the Lord what he is doing in this person in front of you, and only when his love has motivated you and his Spirit has compelled you, begin to speak. Of course, this is easier said than done! Are there any situations in your life right now with friends or family where you may need to *stop* assuming that you know what they need and start asking the Lord what he wants for them?

One time Jeremy saw a man jogging and felt prompted to share the gospel with him, even though it seemed he was pretty busy, out for his run. Jeremy stopped the man and said, "I really don't want to stop you from your jog, but I have a message that may be the most important thing you've ever heard." The man stopped and listened as Jeremy gave a simple, almost unfortunately reductionistic outline of the gospel. At the end of that conversation, the man, who was jogging in place the *entire* time, stopped jogging and started crying and said, "I have been praying for months for the Lord to send someone to me to explain these things. I have had so much confusion and chaos in my spiritual life, but today you have provided all I need to know. I want to give my life to Jesus right now." Wait on the Lord and learn to be silent when necessary; and when the Lord puts it on your heart to do something, do it. Jeremy didn't want to bother that man; yet in that situation, he knew the Lord was leading.

INCARNATIONAL LIVING TOOLS

Tools are the adaptable, practical methods that light our way. Like a handheld torch, tools illuminate specific areas of need or challenge, guiding our actions. Not every practice will be suitable for every situation. Therefore, careful discernment is crucial in selecting the right tool for the task. Once a particular tool effectively reveals solutions, we can apply it with increasing diligence and frequency, focusing our efforts where they are most needed.

Tool #1: The Contextualization Process

When seeking to be truly incarnational, we must study the culture around us and begin the hard work of faithful discernment regarding the context that we are in. The following categories are helpful for understanding the culture around us:

- **Linguistic insight:** What does the language of a people tell us about their values, perceptions, and actions?
- **Cultural texts or artifacts:** What are the objects and cultural goods used by a people, and how do these objects continue to shape them?
- **Beliefs:** What are the values and perceptions that shape people's worldviews and inform/compel their actions?
- **Causes:** What is the central cause (or causes) that people orient themselves around/toward?
- **Measurements:** How do people measure their outcomes/goals/ achievements as worthwhile?
- **Rituals and methodologies:** What are the actions and rituals that embody people's deeper beliefs?
- **Plans:** How do people plan their intentional methods and approaches toward their centralizing mission/values?[17]

These insights are worth considering when you look at your own church or even your smallest group of friends. Yet, for our purposes now, let's consider the broader culture around us. Are we attentive to the culture we are in? If we are, how do we seek to understand, engage, and react to it? By God's grace, we are given the tools to affirm that which is affirmable, challenge that which needs to be challenged, and respond appropriately (not over-reacting). At times we are called to live within or alongside the culture and, at others, as distinct and away from the culture—there is an appointed time for everything.

---

[17] In their book *The Church as Movement*, JR Woodward and Dan White Jr. present similar concepts using the LAAMMPS acrostic for analyzing culture. See Woodward and White, *The Church as Movement*, 162.

Tool #2: Relational and Non-Relational

In recent history, it seems some have used the term "relational evangelism" as nothing more than an excuse not to share the gospel. We need to be aware that sharing good news will happen in both relational contexts *and* in non-relational contexts. Both are needed. If we really have good news, then we need to get it out there in whatever ways are truly appropriate, honoring to the Lord and honoring to the people we are loving. There are times when evangelism absolutely must be focused on reaching the masses,[18] times when we must *boldly* proclaim the gospel (always be ready!), and times when we must simply wait on the Lord to save.[19]

Speaking from our experience, we regularly share good news about Jesus both with strangers and friends. The key is knowing that *both* need to hear the gospel, and sometimes we need to be silent and wait on his movement. We have met a number of "strangers" who ended up becoming followers of Jesus because the Holy Spirit worked between us during a random encounter. We have also seen friends and long-term relationships impacted by the steady stream of love from Christ into us and then into them.

Tool #3: Discover *Your* Evangelistic Style

Many people think that evangelism is *only one* particular way of sharing the gospel, or they think of the door-to-door evangelism model (which is still quite effective when done *appropriately* in *certain* cultures). But because of these misconceptions, many people say things like, "I am not an evangelist. That isn't my gift." But when is someone without the gift of mercy ever justified in *not* showing mercy? Who, without the gift of teaching, is ever justified in not teaching someone in need? Who,

---

[18] Jesus preached to over five thousand at once in Mark 6, and Peter and Paul also preached to large crowds.

[19] Lamentations 3:21–26 has a lot to say about waiting for the saving work of the Lord to be enacted. It says he is *good* to those who wait on him. And yes, even within the context of Lamentations, the principles in that chapter are eternal and also apply to incarnational living and waiting on the Lord to work in the hearts of those around us.

without the gift of evangelism, is ever justified in *not* being willing to share good news of life with another?

When individuals discover their particular style of evangelism, it can often release them to evangelize with greater love and freedom than ever before. For example, in *The Permanent Revolution*, Alan Hirsch and Tim Catchim give us a beautiful and liberating understanding of *how* different people approach sharing Jesus with those around them.[20] Just as different emphases create different personality types, so each type will proclaim the gospel differently; but each type is needed, *and* each type is biblical. All the types must proclaim Jesus as good news. (If there is *no* proclamation, then there is no telling of good news; and if that isn't happening, then you can't really call it evangelism.)

There are four common *practices* within evangelism, and the unique combination of these practices leads to four common evangelistic *styles.*

The *practices* are: 1) heavy and frequent proclamation, 2) event orientation, 3) intentional presence (in people's lives), and 4) deep understanding of process. Jesus did all four of these: He proclaimed frequently and publicly; he saw events and circumstances as opportunities to plant seeds in people's lives; he had intentional presence in leading the Twelve to follow him;[21] and he was process oriented—just look at his parables!

All of these practices will attract people to Jesus, but you may lean toward some methods more than others. Knowing this paradigm will help you discern your particular *style* of evangelism: *converser, convincer, investor,* or *inviter.*

The *converser* mostly practices proclamation and process orientation. They can't help proclaiming often and frequently, and they see

---

[20] Alan Hirsch and Tim Catchim, *The Permanent Revolution: Apostolic Imagination and Practice for the 21st Century Church* (Jossey-Bass, 2012).

[21] The great question is, "At what point did they have 'saving faith'?" Perhaps it was different for each of the Twelve! Think of Thomas in John 20, and then think of Peter, and then Nathaniel— all seemed to "get it" about Jesus at different times, but Jesus was present in their lives for three years, patiently waiting on their transformation with great hope.

themselves as planting seeds that will take *time* and *phases* of growth before they are ready to be reaped.

The *convincer* is the one we typically think of when we consider evangelists: one who proclaims the gospel frequently and always aims to move people appropriately to the event of conversion. Unfortunately, this is the only way that most people have historically seen evangelism, so it has limited other personality types from being freed up to do evangelism in their own way (which would ultimately result in personal, global, and movemental impact). Yet, we mustn't react negatively to this particular style but rather help others to grow in their understanding of their style of evangelism.

The *investor* is focused on the process of planting seeds, watering those seeds, and *waiting*, while also remaining loyally *immersed* in the lives of those being loved.

The *inviter* is one who understands that presence is needed and understands the dynamics of teamwork for the sake of creating helpful events and environments for those who are beginning to seek Christ.[22]

Remember: Jesus practiced all four of these methods with perfect wisdom, harmony, and love. We would do well to remember this, whatever method is most fitting for us.

You may find that you move from one of these styles to another over the course of your life. You may also discover that there are times to "put on the hat" of a particular style that you are less comfortable with. This is the Lord stretching you into the spiritual maturity of learning to discern his leading. Which style fits you best in this season of your life? Which style makes you feel most uncomfortable? Be ok with any discomfort for now. Focus on how the Lord is leading you forward to be light in the darkness and salt (a preserving agent) in this world (Matthew 5:16ff).

As you follow Jesus, remember: He shared the good news with Nicodemus by telling him that he could be born again. He shared the good news with the woman at the well by telling her about the water of life (the Holy Spirit). He shared good news with the woman

---

22 Hirsch and Catchim, *The Permanent Revolution*, 39.

accused of adultery by telling her, "Neither do I condemn you. Go and sin no more." He shared the good news with Thomas by allowing him to put his hand on his scars and see his resurrected body. He shared the good news with crowds by his public preaching. He shared the good news with many others by doing miracles and ministering to their needs. These are just a few of Jesus' methods. Since Jesus used multiple styles of evangelism, it frees us to be who we are as he molds us into new creations! Keep following him into his kingdom practices.

Tool #4: Power Evangelism

Given the debates, the reaction, and over-reaction to the concept of power evangelism, we tread carefully. I recommend that you pick up a newer edition of *Power Evangelism* by John Wimber and read it for yourself before you judge it.[23] Many have taken the book too far. Others have seen the imbalanced response and reacted with heavy criticism or fear of the implications of abuse of some of the concepts in the book. But when we've been able to navigate these tensions, we have witnessed some extremely powerful moments where the Spirit works as we simply ask someone, "How can I pray for you?"

Despite abuses of spiritual gifts, we are all still called to faithfully pursue a lifestyle of actively and intentionally following Jesus. To follow him means to be attentive to his ways and then live accordingly. Some of his ways while living on earth involved miraculous activity, and he has told us that he sent his Holy Spirit to indwell in us (John 14:16). Not only this, but our lives are hidden with Christ in God (Colossians 3:3). We are confronted with the fact that his miraculous power is a constant in our lives. How much more miraculous can you get than to be indwelt with the Holy Spirit or to be hidden with Christ in God? Therefore, it should be normative for us to expect miraculous activity that brings glory to the name of Jesus Christ.

---

[23] Wimber, *Power Evangelism*.

Power evangelism can be summed up as asking people how you can pray for them, and then immediately praying for them (and with them) on the spot.

It's that simple. Expect God to sometimes show up in amazing ways, and also realize that he may not choose to visibly display his supernatural power, doing seemingly nothing that we can see. He simply calls us to keep waiting patiently on him. We pray and obey and watch and wait.

In our experience, when we have asked a person how we can pray for them, we have seen the Lord do incredible things that just don't fit into our previous "religious" experience or prior theological confines. We pray and follow as those who trust him to work in this world because we understand that he is sovereign and loving.

Tool #5: Gospel Listening

In *The Tangible Kingdom,* Halter and Smay do an excellent job describing an aspect of humble contextualization: gospel listening. Gospel listening requires us to stop thinking that we know all the answers and that our agenda is the highest priority in our relationships. Gospel listening requires that we *begin* listening to where there is brokenness, hurt, pain, and desire in the lives of those around us. It is about becoming attentive to the ways that someone's life *already* shows how the gospel is vital for them; we look for the elements of "creation, fall, redemption, and restoration" in a person's life. Sometimes we hear them speak of a "creation" phase—when things were good, when life seemed abundant. Other times we hear them speak of a period of "fall," or curse, breakdown, loss, or suffering. We identify with this because we have also experienced these times and know how the gospel fits into a world that is suffering. We hear another person speaking of hope for forgiveness or reconciliation in a relationship or speaking of their guilt, and we know that they are in need of the healing that comes from "redemption." We hear them deal with fear, doubt, and unease in this world, and we know they are longing for "restoration."

Commit to listen to a friend this week—listen for *how* the gospel speaks directly into their life. Then go home and pray about how you might speak into their life at a future point. Unless the Spirit moves you to speak immediately, practice self-control and patience and wait on the Lord to see how he may want you to invest spiritually in that person after considering how the gospel will speak most directly to them in their weakness and brokenness.

Tool #6: Three Stories of Good News

"Ok, but *how* do I share the gospel with people?" Let's get super practical. It's this simple—there are three stories that need to be engaged when sharing the gospel with a friend:

1. What is *their* story? (Here you do gospel listening.)
2. What is *your* story? (How have you been broken and hurt [from creation to fall]? How has Jesus redeemed and restored you? How have you experienced the reality that Jesus is trustworthy, and his ways are good?)
3. What is *Jesus'* story?

Tool #7: Discerning Your Missional Lanes

As we follow Jesus in his mission, we must discern the particular context in which the Lord is calling us to serve. One person may be great at reaching their neighbors but not as great at reaching a certain people group in their city, but someone else may be excellent at reaching that people group and struggle with caring for their actual neighbors. This is where the distinction of "missional lanes" helps to set us free to discern the way forward:

- **Neighbors:** This generally means neighbors next door, coworkers, or students, etc. How is Jesus being incarnated in your life in your neighborhood?
- **Networks:** These involve people who come together around

certain activities or affinities. You may play a sport, or be a gamer, or belong to a certain club. These networks or social circles may make perfect sense for you to focus on. How does Jesus want to be known among your friends?

- **People groups:** You may have a burden of love and care for a specific people group in your city (those with disabilities, or internationals, the homeless, wealthy business owners, etc.). What does good news look like for these groups?
- **Places:** There may be geographic areas that are in particular need. You may see a neighborhood that has been destroyed by drugs, or an area that has had recent flooding and needs some help, or a brand-new development where everyone is moving in with new hopes and dreams. Are you drawn to a particular location where Jesus wants his kingdom to reign for his glory?

Tool #8: Hospitality as Mission

Whatever your missional lane, never forget that hospitality is a vital form of mission. St. Patrick is a good example. In George C. Hunter's classic book *The Celtic Way of Evangelism*, we read how Patrick of the Celt's made his way into northern Europe and set up monastic communities along the road to help those who were traveling.[24]

These communities had an "availability" ethos: They were ready to give food, ready to host, ready to love, ready to help, ready to nurture, and ready to minister to all who came to their door. Their mission was to stay put for a while, incarnate *love* in an area, and then multiply out to other areas. Some have said that the Lord used Patrick to set an apostolic church-planting movement in motion that impacted millions in northern Europe and helped lay the groundwork for Christianity's continued global impact.

Hospitality as mission can be one of the most transformative elements in our ministries today. All true missional activity will be

---

[24] George C. Hunter, *The Celtic Way of Evangelism: How Christianity Can Reach the West ... AGAIN*, 10th ed. (Abingdon Press, 2011).

encompassed by a discipleship-oriented aim and permeated by love. Hospitality only flows forth from a heart of love. Hospitality means bringing someone into a place, affirming and loving them as they are, and showing them dignity by inviting them to *be* with you. Notice how hospitality is seen in three of the most important elements of the redemptive narrative:

- **Creation:** God creates a place, then invites humans to live in that place with him. This is hospitality as primary *missio Dei* (mission of God).
- **Christ:** After we rejected God's hospitality, he sent his Son that there might be peace established between us and God. We are invited to be a new creation and to have a place in his adopted family. Through Christ, we are welcomed into the Family of God! This is hospitality as central renewal and redemptive *missio Dei*.
- **Eternal State:** God has prepared a table and a house for us to live with him into eternity. We are welcomed into his kingdom starting now and into his eternal city for a marriage feast with the Lamb![25] This is hospitality as covenantal and eternal *missio Dei*.

Throughout Scripture, there is a pattern of us being told to do or be something because *God* has done or is something. For example: Be holy because he is holy (Leviticus 19:2 and the writings of Peter), love because he has loved (1 John and many other places), and forgive because he has forgiven (Jesus tells us to do this, as does Paul). The model is clear: We do because *God* has done; we are because *he* is. God's hospitality in mission toward us motivates us to be imitators of him. Let's welcome those around us into our homes, lives, awkward places, and fun places. Let's bring people along with in the mundane and the exciting. May our lives become hospitality as mission.

---

[25] See creation in Genesis 1–2; Jesus' example in John 1:12, 3:16, and Romans 5:8–11; and our eternal state in Revelation 21–22.

Tool #9: Marketplace Christianity

Rather than idolizing the concept of "full-time ministry," we need people to begin practicing the presence of God and seeing how they are *already being paid to be a full-time missionary where they work!* Imagine you are a missionary in your workplace—you are funded to be there, and you get to be alongside these precious image-bearers every day. You get to plant seeds in certain people that perhaps you would never meet in any other way.[26] *We need missionaries in the marketplace!*

Tool #10: People of Peace

In recent years, the "person of peace" principle Jesus referred to in Luke 10 has become enlarged and expanded by the observations of many in missional circles. Those of us who have been focusing on neighborhoods, people groups, geographic areas, and affinity groups for the sake of contextualizing the gospel in those arenas have often noted that there are sometimes "gatekeepers" in these places. These people can effectively open the door for many more connections. For example, when we moved to Richmond, Virginia, one neighbor ended up introducing us to about fifty people across the city, and many of those then brought us into their extended circles. The neighbor later left the area, but for years afterward, we continued to deepen friendships with those with whom she had connected us. Malcolm Gladwell in *The Tipping Point* points out that epidemic movements occur when three types of people are mobilized:

- **Salespeople**—people who are contagious in spreading values, interests, or thoughts and who are excellent at convincing others naturally.

---

[26] Robert Fraser's book *Marketplace Christianity* is the best book we have read on this subject. If you feel called to the workplace, or called to entrepreneurship in the broader market, then please read this book. Robert Fraser, *Marketplace Christianity: Discovering the Kingdom Purpose of the Marketplace* (New Grid Books, 2011).

- **Mavens**—those with unusually high amounts of random but trustworthy knowledge, who can give uniquely insightful advice and information in just the right way.
- **Connectors**—people who can open up entirely new social circles or are connected to a wide range of people groups.[27]

We would do well to consider who these people may be in our lives and then love them well, for the seeds of love planted in them have the potential to spread to many, *many* more people.

"People of peace" in modern missional literature have been likened to the "connectors" that Malcolm Gladwell refers to. Yet a person of peace can also be as simple as the local woman who happens to know all the neighbors—and also happens to know eccentric details about every garden in the neighborhood, as some in Richmond seem to! Jesus basically said that while the disciples were on mission, if someone welcomed them in, they should let their peace stay there and allow the Lord to work in that place; but if someone rejected them, they should move on.

Jeremy experienced this overseas in India, where one tribe rejected him and his team entirely, chasing them from the village with weapons in their hands. But a neighboring village took them in, gave them a meal, and asked them to share with the village elders. The team shared with the elders, and the elders fell down on the ground weeping, saying, "Lord, have mercy on me! Save me!" They were *absolutely horrified* to hear that the Almighty God's Incarnate Son, Jesus, was crucified. Jeremy will never forget the look on the elder's faces when they heard those words. But when he explained the resurrection, they were thrilled. The elders put their confidence in Christ, and the entire village proclaimed their trust in Jesus! Jeremy and his team stayed there, did more work, and ate more food. Clearly, some of these villages showed great grace in welcoming them. After this, the team focused on the villages that had connections to their national workers. This ensured that upon

---

[27] Malcolm Gladwell, *The Tipping Point: How Little Things Can Make a Big Difference* (Little, Brown and Company, 2000), 38, 59, 70.

arrival, the team was received by people who already knew and had welcomed their colleagues. The team saw maximum impact when they followed a person of peace into the villages where those relationships were already established.

Woodward and White in *The Church as Movement* give helpful observations about people of peace. They point to Thom Wolf and Erwin McManus at Mosaic in California who describe people of peace as follows: "They are receptive to us, have a reputation in this place, and they refer us to other circles."[28] Woodward and White also highlight Bob and Mary Hopkins' paradigm for identifying a person of peace:

- **Perception:** Perceive where a person of peace is at spiritually, and where their *oikos* (household/people group) is at spiritually. Are they open or closed to spiritual conversation? If they are not thirsty, give them salt; if they are thirsty, give them living water.
- **Passing or permanent:** Is this a passing relationship (someone who is about to leave town but still invites you into their friendship group) or permanent (someone who might persevere alongside you relationally for a long time)? This enables you to have insight into how you shape your missional approach.
- **Proclamation and presence:** Discern to what extent they are open to direct proclamation as well as your loving presence in their lives. (Review the points made previously in this chapter about evangelistic style and proclamation, presence, event, and process.)
- **Power and preparation:** Citing John Wimber (*Power Evangelism*), Woodward and White state that we must consider how the power of God may need to be played out in this person's life, and we "ask God to intervene in a dramatic way through healing prayer, a prophetic word, or a Spirit-inspired dream." Yet we also consider how the Lord may want to use us to prepare the soil in their lives by planting, cultivating, watering, etc.[29]

---

[28] Woodward and White, *The Church as Movement*, 200.

[29] Woodward and White, *The Church as Movement*, 202.

Tool #11: Contextualization

Some people use contextualization in an extremely rational way, relying too much on sociological paradigms, and it becomes just another way to "lean on their own understanding." On the opposite end of the spectrum, people who *never* contextualize either run around bashing people with the gospel in ways that hurt others and the testimony of Christ, or fail to ask what would be the best approach in their context that is most honoring to the Holy Spirit. In the name of following the Holy Spirit, many atrocious mistakes have been made. So let us carefully honor the Spirit of God by observing how he has made us—as intellectual beings who have the capacity to observe our surroundings, observe the culture around us, and then minister to people appropriately. But let us also allow the Holy Spirit to lead us to trust him more than our logical systems at times (as in the case of evangelism to the jogger mentioned previously).

In global missions, contextualization has also been a way for some people to create syncretistic or pluralistic abuses of the gospel—mixing other religious ideas together and ultimately distorting the message away from the biblical gospel toward some sort of new-age conglomeration of thought. As a result, some are offended even at the word "contextualization" because they fear that a bastardization of the gospel is about to ensue.[30]

But contextualization is about examining a culture and a people, understanding them well. It requires that you understand the "why" or the motivations of people for their various actions. Then you take the unchanging message of the gospel—Jesus is trustworthy and can be entrusted with your *whole* life, and because of his life, death, and resurrection, you can follow him *now* into his life and eternal kingdom and salvation—and you find the ways that the gospel most appropriately speaks to this people.

---

[30] That being the case, the best resource for anyone wanting to jump deeply and appropriately into contextualization is Timothy Keller's *Center Church*. It will open many doors for you to continue exploring this massive (and we mean *massive*) subject in current missiological writings.

We mentioned earlier that Jesus shared the good news in a variety of ways (John 3–4), and he gave us some insight as to why he interacted with people in different ways ("I only do what I see the Father doing"). We know that Jesus had supernatural insight into people's lives and issues, but we also see that Jesus dealt with people according to what was appropriate in each situation. Jesus understood the context, the person, and what would be the wisest way of communicating in each moment. In Christ are hidden *all* the treasures of wisdom and knowledge (Colossians 2:3), so we can be certain that he spoke with wisdom to every person he interacted with.

Whether you call that contextualization or not, Jesus understood how to operate in wisdom. Let us learn to use wisdom and listen to the guidance of the Holy Spirit.[31] Paul famously contextualized the gospel in Athens in Acts 17. Paul spoke differently to those in Athens than he did to those in other contexts. He used concepts and practices from their culture in order to influence them appropriately, and he observed the cultural and spiritual context before he acted. This is contextualization.

Bringing this into our day, another vital tool for contextualization comes from Woodward and White, asking questions of the context we are trying to reach. It is framed around the word NEAR:

- **Narrative:** What story is our neighborhood/network/town/city calling us to embody? How does the gospel speak to this?
- **Ethics:** How do people in our neighborhood/network/town/city define success and appropriate lifestyles? What does that say about their deeper values? How does the gospel speak into this?
- **Associations:** What primary organizations (and cultural forces/identity groups) are shaping people's identity and destiny in our neighborhood/network/town/city? How does the gospel speak into these associations?

---

[31] These are one and the same, but depending on your denominational background, you may have heard more focus placed on wisdom or more on the Spirit. Learn to see them as working hand-in-hand, and you will experience more and more freedom!

- **Rituals:** What core practices do people engage in that shape their identity and sense of purpose in life in our neighborhoods/networks/town/city? How does the gospel speak to these rituals? Does it confront some? Affirm others?[32]

Beyond these reasons, we must embrace gospel contextualization in maturity and humility.

IT'S SCRIPTURAL. IT'S RATIONAL. IT'S TRANSFORMATIONAL.

Incarnational living—*being* the message of the good news while *speaking* the message of the good news while *doing* the message of the good news—is explicitly demonstrated across the pages of the Bible.

Rationally, the methods here make more sense as you consider humanity. How do you truly honor a person? How do you express urgent, life-altering matters to someone without adding offense? One friend once said, "Look, the ship is sinking. I need to tell people, and it doesn't matter how I tell them. They just need to know." But that in itself is a logical fallacy (non sequitur). No matter *how* urgent and important the message is, we can easily do more harm than good if we don't use common sense and wisdom in our approach to communicating it. We can also do harm if we don't allow the Spirit of God to guide our actions and make clear *how* we are to communicate the good news. The ancient Proverbs tell us that the wise person gives thought to a word before saying it, thereby adding judiciousness to his/her lips. What a beautiful insight! If the ship is sinking, you can express the urgency, but you don't have to grab them by the throat and shake them while you tell them.

We have explored several tools in this chapter, and we have personally seen all four major styles of evangelism (investor, inviter, converser, and convincer) be effective when done well and directed by the Holy Spirit. Overall, we have more often seen deep spiritual realities

---

[32] Woodward and White, *The Church as Movement*, 193.

shift in people's lives because of being incarnational and present with them, investing slowly over a period of time. We don't bash any one model, but we practice deference. Transformation increases from that point onward.

4

MOVEMENT WISDOM
Being Movemental

 KEY IDEAS

- Worshiping in spirit and in truth (John 4) is essential to life in Christ and to spreading his movement. Worship draws worshipers into his kingdom.
- Think about "movement" as a stewardship and relational partnership between you and God.
- Disciples make disciples who make disciples—this creates movement.
- Scripture provides a constitutional template for understanding polycentric leadership as part of our identity as a "royal priesthood" in Ephesians 4 (APEST).
- This chapter contains tools that will help us honor the Lord's heart for his global and historic movement (which includes us, as his royal priesthood). Remember his tender, compassionate, and loving heart as you engage with being movemental.

 ## SEE FOR YOURSELF

Look at the book of Acts, considering its overall flow, and ask yourself: What are the elements of the movement of God? What patterns of intentionality do you see in the early church leaders? To go further, read through Ecclesiastes or Proverbs. Ask the Lord what he wants to reveal to you about wisdom, then consider that in light of his mission in this world. Or read through Mark and ask yourself: How did Jesus' life reflect his mission and lend itself toward the spreading of a movement?

 ## MOVEMENT WISDOM FOUNDATIONS

Foundations are our unshakable core map, charting the terrain. Foundations provide the rock-solid theological principles that remain constant, regardless of the specific location or context we find ourselves in. They equip and prepare us for the journey, ensuring we have a reliable understanding of the fundamental landscape.

Foundation #1: Worship

True worship is a heart of adoration toward the Lord. True worship doesn't require music, though it can sometimes involve it. True worship involves a heart that is struck with the reality of the glory and love of the Triune God. True worship is a reality that you carry with you in your heart and in the atmosphere around you. It is an all-encompassing awareness and delight of who God is as we are in his presence.

In John 4:23, Jesus mentioned that the time was coming when true worshipers would worship the Father "in spirit and in truth." (How beautiful and fitting of his kingdom way that Jesus would reveal such a truth to a Samaritan outcast just before her finding salvation in him.) We are told in Genesis 4:26 that people began to call on the name of the Lord. But even before the time when people began to call on the name of the Lord (an event that followed the Lord's response to Cain's plea regarding his brother Abel's murder), Abel had demonstrated a heart of true worship by bringing a sacrifice to God (v. 3). Since the beginning, we can see worship as something ingrained deep in humanity.

Ecclesiastes 3:11 tells us that eternity is written on our hearts, and in the first sin of Adam and Eve, they were, in fact, worshiping something other than God. We could say that everything comes back to worship. And everything true starts with true and appropriately directed worship (adoration, respect, honor, and gratitude). Everything false starts when worship flows in the wrong direction.

When we worship, we join in the history of those who have called upon the name of Yahweh. Yet we connect ourselves with the future of worship as well—those who will stand around the throne day and night, crying out, "Holy, Holy, Holy …" (Revelation 4:8). As we read this, we might ask what is happening in this scene? What do we learn about worship from this moment in the throne room?

Jesus declared to the Samaritan woman that true worship was a coming and pervasive reality. It was on his heart when he purified the temple (Matthew 21:12). It was in his words when he surrendered his life to the Father (Luke 23:46). This true worship was in the heart of the thief on the cross when he asked Jesus to remember him in paradise (Luke 23:42). In the Great Commission, Jesus ushered in and declared a global movement of appropriately placed adoration toward the Father, Son, and Holy Spirit (Matthew 28:18–20). Therefore, true Trinitarian worship is interwoven with the movement of disciple-making.

In this chapter, we are going to talk about movement dynamics and tools for facilitating the stewardship of a movement. But if we were to read this or do these things *without* true worship as the end goal, we would miss the point. Jesus is calling new eternal worshipers into the Father's kingdom, and he asks us to go fishing with him for these new worshipers and to cultivate and procure a people who will connect with the deepest element of our purpose—to know him, to delight in him, to take immense pleasure from being in his presence.

Look at the growth of the human population throughout history. Early on, people were limited to a few locations around the world, and ancient peoples were located in only a few time zones. But as the human race expanded, humanity reached a point where it was present in every time zone for the first time in world history. So, on a twenty-four-hour rotation of the earth, there was always someone sleeping, always someone eating their first meal of the day, always someone eating their last meal of the day, etc. This required expansive growth of the human population. And some time after that, and perhaps no one knows when, there was *at least one worshiper of Jesus in every time zone.* We can imagine a unique celebration in heaven at that moment, when the angels and those around the throne paused and noticed: Today is the day that there has begun to be ceaseless praise and worship from humans on planet earth! The angels were already worshiping nonstop. Creation itself was already worshiping nonstop (Psalm 19). But, if you could measure worship, if it had a physical substance or volume, then you could say that on that day, the volume of worship being poured out to the Father increased substantially. We can also assume that the forces of darkness were terrified on that day to see such a procession of triumphant victory in the kingdom of heaven. Well, worship has only increased since then! Today, at any given point around the globe, there are worshipers of Jesus adoring him and lifting him up. We bring forth the deeper realities of his kingdom when we worship in spirit and in truth. We are living in this day when nonstop praise is offered from the hearts of men and women around the world on a constant basis. If this kind of worship isn't present in our movements, then we must ask what kind of movement we are participating in.

Foundation #2: Stewardship

You can focus on Christ and live with him, follow and make followers of him, and then live incarnationally and missionally for his sake and reach others with his love. But if we truly want to accomplish those specific tasks, we need to think in terms of what is going to lend itself to a global movement and what is not.

For example, we can sit down with a new believer and explore Jesus with them through the book of John. This will enable them to go and teach someone else from the book of John almost immediately. That activity lends itself to multiplication. We personally saw this happen with a girl we met in Cape Town in South Africa. After we shared the message of God's kingdom with her, she had a transformative experience with Christ. She immediately went and shared these same elements with two of her friends at home, which resulted in them both choosing faith in Jesus. Later on, the three of them formed a spiritual formation group that met multiple times a week to read Scripture and learn how to live a life similar to Jesus'.

As another approach, we could take that new follower of Jesus and require her to get a master's degree before she makes disciples. Or we could require her to complete heavy training that hinders the movement by delaying the disciple-making impact of this potential discipler. Think about it—train someone in the gospel of John and enable them to multiply, *or* require them to undergo intensive years of training (possibly with great financial expenditure) before encouraging them to multiply. One of these is sustainable; the other is not.

This is where we see that movement is a stewardship issue. God controls the resources of time, energy, money, people, space, etc., but he entrusts these to us to either waste or use wisely. So, if we think about how a movement happens and study ways of allowing the message of Christ to become widespread, we must use wisdom to honor the Spirit of God in his global disciple-making movement.

Foundation #3: The Kingdom of Heaven

In many theological circles, you will hear little about "the kingdom of heaven," yet Matthew and Luke are dominated by this language. It has been revolutionary in our lives to study the kingdom of heaven; after all, Jesus says to seek this kingdom first and God's righteousness, and then everything else we need will be brought into our lives (Matthew 6:33). But it wasn't until our mid-twenties that we could give a solid definition of the kingdom of God. This wasn't due to any failure on the part of our teachers or family but rather of the time it took for these truths to sink in deeply in our lives.

In *The Tangible Kingdom Primer*, Halter and Smay demonstrate how they would disciple people primarily by talking about the kingdom of God.[1] The mission organization Forge America (of which Hugh Halter is a part) is a network that is also aimed at helping every Jesus-follower embrace a deeper understanding of the kingdom of heaven. The Lord used Halter and some of the people in Forge America to open our eyes to see the parables of Jesus in an entirely new light. Then we read Dallas Willard's *The Divine Conspiracy* and began to see even greater depths to the reality of the kingdom of heaven.[2] If Jesus said that the kingdom of God is the thing to seek first, how many of us have ever actually known what that means? Willard is often quoted as saying that the kingdom of God is everything that falls under the reign and rule of God's values and intentions. The kingdom of God is everything that is moving in line with his intent. Anything that moves against the Lord is from another kingdom. God's kingdom is an eternal kingdom, with eternal values; and he desires to bring forth from the human race a set of people who will join him in loving community and reign with him into eternity. Jesus unpacks so many powerful truths in his parables. We encourage you to seek his kingdom by studying these and considering what his teaching reveals about our world, our lives, and the patterns of life that he has for us, both here and into eternity.

In *Center Church*, Keller mentions the kingdom being an "already but not yet" kingdom.[3] It is present and people are pressing into it everywhere (as Jesus said in Luke 16:16), yet this kingdom is not fully consummated, for it eagerly awaits a final glorification (Romans 8:18). It is a "forward-back" kingdom in the sense that the first shall be last and the last shall be first (Matthew 20:16); and if anyone wants to gain life, that person must first be willing to entirely lose their life (Matthew 16:25); and while Jesus has already been resurrected, we have not yet experienced the fullness of resurrection, etc. It is an upside-down

---

[1]   Halter and Smay, *The Tangible Kingdom Primer*.

[2]   Dallas Willard, *The Divine Conspiracy: Rediscovering Our Hidden Life in God* (HarperCollins, 1998).

[3]   Keller, *Center Church*, 46–48.

kingdom where the king came and became a servant. It is an inside-out kingdom where to truly be clean, we start with the inside issues and only then can we begin to deal with our outside behaviors and actions (Matthew 23:25). These unique tensions create space for us to build faith as disciples, to live in the eternal realities of the kingdom, to adopt an entirely new way of thinking, and to value with an entirely new value system.

Foundation #4: Epidemic Growth

Many in movement thinking have asked: How did the early church go from a few hundred followers of Jesus (post-resurrection) to spreading throughout the entire Roman Empire within a couple of hundred years? That was epidemic growth—a contagious, Holy Spirit movement directed toward widespread growth. Some ask how the church in China went from such a small number of believers to tens of millions (and hundreds of millions according to some estimates). Others look at church-planting movements in Indonesia, Mongolia, Peru, Brazil, India, Zimbabwe, Kenya, Tanzania, South Africa, Nigeria, and Ghana, among immigrant groups, and other viral discipleship movements and ask these same questions: What is lending a hand to movements, and what is not?[4]

For those who may say, "Let the Holy Spirit be in charge of creating and growing movements," we would challenge them to think about the same principle in relation to loving your neighbor. We might think we can let the Holy Spirit be in charge, yet Jesus still commands us to love our neighbor and make disciples of all the nations. So rather than using theological dodges to avoid responsibility for thinking about his global movement, let us lend ourselves to the questions of responsible stewardship of his resources.

The kingdom of heaven is like leaven (Matthew 13:33). The kingdom

---

[4] David Garrison's book *Church Planting Movements: How God is Redeeming a Lost World* (Wigtake Resources, 2003), is a fascinating read on these topics, and Hirsch's *The Forgotten Way* is a genius classic on movement dynamics and thinking.

of heaven is like a seed that grows into a tree (Matthew 13:31–32). The kingdom of heaven is like compound growth. To neglect these ideas is to miss out on the nature of the kingdom of heaven in action, taking on a life of its own (as Willard said). We have seen movements in action in Kenya, Tanzania, South Africa, Zimbabwe, Lesotho, Nigeria, Ghana, and Peru; and in other places we have personally planted churches that planted churches that planted churches *beyond our ability to control*. That is compound growth. Exponential growth. We could call this the eighth wonder of the world—the compound growth of the kingdom of God. It is alive and well in the body of Christ, and we can participate in it, thanks to the gracious hospitality of the Father inviting us into his mission with him. As Alan Hirsch has often mentioned, a seed doesn't only carry the potential for a single tree but for a forest.

Foundation #5: Contagious

For something to go viral, it must be contagious ... sticky. Malcolm Gladwell refers to these ideas in *The Tipping Point*, as do authors Dan and Chip Heath in *Made to Stick*.[5] Whenever social epidemics happen, there are typically a few key factors: Perhaps it is a logo or work of art that so perfectly represents the values that it *sticks* in people's minds. Or a mantra or phrase that just connects with people. In fashion, an accessible and small change can make a big difference. In political movements, it can be as simple as a word. In film analysis, an unnoticed film can suddenly become a cult classic because of certain simple, but genius, dynamics that are quotable, memorable, and unique. In literature, it can be a main idea that is so clear and *ready* for the people of the time to embrace it. In music, it is a beat that gets stuck in people's minds. Often, the "sticky" or contagious element wakes us up to something that was dormant.[6]

---

[5] Gladwell, *The Tipping Point*, 133–134; Dan and Chip Heath, *Made to Stick: Why Some Ideas Take Hold and Others Come Unstuck* (Arrow, 2008), 16–17.

[6] Time and space don't permit us to list all of the examples of "sticky" factors. Some helpful resources include: 1) Kevin J. Vanhoozer's book *Everyday Theology: How to Read Cultural Texts and Interpret Trends* (Baker Academic, 2007) is useful to gather some tools for studying

Jesus spoke contagiously. His most famous sermon isn't actually that long! He told pithy parables that were memorable, and some were just a single phrase. He summed up the Law and the Prophets with two commands: love God, love others. He commissioned a global movement with one short exhortation. Jesus was clearly a steward of his words, knowing when to speak, when to remain silent, and how to say just the right amount needed to drop the seed into the soil.

Typically, cultural trends that spread start on the sidelines, with people on the fringes who directly influence the mainstream or center of the culture. Marketers *study* people on the margins to see what they are doing as a sign of what is coming culturally in the near future. Then marketers jump on it and help spread it so they can profit from it. If advertisers can get this, then surely, we can follow the Holy Spirit and into a place of seeding the viral kingdom everywhere we go.

Foundation #6: Church-Planting Movements

In studies of church-planting movements (CPMs), David Garrison, among others, has noted some additional elements that might challenge our approaches to how we do church.[7]

These CPMs don't always look like the typical or traditional churches that we might think of in developed nations. Ying Kai's model of "Training for Trainers" (T4T) went global and produced over one million small discipleship groups. Kai calls these groups "churches," and technically they are gatherings of believers, as where believers gather, the body of Christ (aka: the church) is spontaneously present.

A key concern for some church leaders regarding church-planting movements is the potential for untrained individuals to form cults. Obviously, this can happen with any church, small or large. Others

---

movements, trends, epidemics, and cultural texts, and 2) Halter and Smay's *The Tangible Kingdom* (different from *The Tangible Kingdom Primer*) to read about some of the ways that contagious ideas have helped spread the good news to people's hearts. Hugh Halter and Matt Smay, *The Tangible Kingdom: Creating Incarnational Community* (Jossey-Bass, 2008).

7 Garrison, *Church Planting Movements*, 49.

are concerned about the dangers of immature people entering into leadership. In the many cases we have seen of movement growth around the world, the Holy Spirit was directing a movement that was *unable* to control its spread. Typically, the founders of these movements couldn't keep track of how fast they were multiplying. They couldn't control how quickly people came to faith and started new groups. It was exponentially reproductive, way beyond their ability to add in an element of "quality control." In these situations, the initiators did their best to provide training in hierarchical forms of concentric circles of influence. Leaders would train those they had discipled, who then replicated the training with their disciples, who would keep passing it down the line. This sounds a little bit like Jesus, focusing on three, twelve, seventy-two, etc.

Movements are messy when they grow quickly! There can be ensuing fallout in superficial movements that haven't produced long-term disciples. So, just because something becomes epidemic doesn't mean it is healthy. Just look at some of the toxic global theological trends that happen all the time (and the internet makes the toxic ideas just as available as the healthy ones).

The hyperactive movement of information and ideas in today's world will likely allow extreme philosophies to radicalize more people than ever before in history. An idea can now go global faster and with more force than just five years ago, and it is only going to speed up. This can be scary, but it can also be a boon for the global movement of the love of Jesus and the message of the kingdom of heaven. We would do well to keep it sticky as Jesus did, keep it simple as Jesus did, and keep planting far and wide (and as creatively as the Spirit of God leads us).

When movements expand healthily, the gospel is contextualized to people groups so effectively that it allows individuals to identify with its message and for it to be embedded in their culture. When movements flourish, the Spirit of the Lord is present and there is freedom. When movements thrive, the DNA is simple. When movements mature and ideas go global, they are not hindered by high-maintenance activities but are facilitated by the natural rhythms of life.

Foundation #7: Movement Killers

As movements spread, how do we take care to steward them well?

Garrison notes that movements expand rapidly *until* people introduce training institutions, which create a clergy/laity divide.[8] Once people get a certain level of training, they expect payment for what they are doing, and this often kills the movement. This is not to say training should not take place, but it should cause us to rethink *how* we do our training. Are we equipping people with the tools needed to be missionaries wherever they go? Or are we reinforcing a "church as an industrial complex" mentality?[9]

Another movement killer is centralizing power and control. In many instances, disciples are making disciples so rapidly that the movement initiators become fearful and try to control what is happening, putting burdens and heavy requirements upon people. Perhaps we are already guilty of this in our churches when we add "extras" to the list of requirements for being a Christian, just as the Pharisees did to the Jewish people in Jesus' day. Do we call people to be culturally "Christian" in the sense of what makes us comfortable, or do we allow people to be followers of Jesus as true disciples? Each of these things—creating a clergy/laity divide and centralizing power—can kill a movement.

 # MOVEMENT WISDOM PARADIGMS

Paradigms are our guiding compass for contextual insight. Paradigms offer a solid framework, acting like a compass that orients us within our context, showing the possible directions we can travel. They shape how we see and interpret our surroundings, guiding the complex work of application.

---

8 Garrison, *Church Planting Movements*, 49–52.

9 As noted by Woodward and White in *The Church as Movement* (page 24) and in their network, The V3 Movement, which coaches and trains local missionaries and church planters. It is essential for coaching and training to call people to return to "church as the movement of the people of God" instead of church as an industrial complex.

Paradigm #1: Removing the Territorial Mindset

A kingdom mindset recognizes that everything is God's territory, rather than churches competing for a "market share" of the Christian community. Instead of worrying about "sheep stealing," we focus on the kingdom of heaven. In his kingdom, God's sheep are in his hand, and no one can take them out! He will continue the work he began in them (Philippians 1:6), and he knows exactly what sort of church or ministry environment will be best for their growth at any given season.

Paradigm #2: Removing False Nationality

Removing a territorial mindset also rescues us from potential imbalances in "patriotism" or nationalism that can deter us from God's goals. In the forty-plus countries we have visited, we have seen ethnocentrism everywhere. No country is without some degree of personal patriotism that can lead to nationalistic self-worship. Even some of the most broken-down countries still boast that their "X" is better than anyone else's in the world. It is natural for people with pride to cultivate pride, not only in themselves but in their relationships at all levels. It's fine to make judgments about one food being better or one culture having certain strengths over others, but when the motive behind our pride or criticisms becomes about a deeper identity/worth issue, we are operating outside of the values of the kingdom of heaven. There is a danger in thinking of our country as "God's country" instead of part of God's world.

Instead of nationalism, consider the global movement centered on Jesus, who has a heart for "all the nations" and every people group. Let us not get distracted with unfit commitments to any earthly kingdom when our true citizenship is as part of God's kingdom.

Paradigm #3: Alternative Kingdom

If we think in terms of the kingdom of heaven—rather than in geopolitical terms—wars, rumors of wars, natural disasters, and political crisis situations take on a different light. We might still grieve over the global situation, but we can begin to ask *new* and different questions. For example, "Father, I see what people are doing there, but what are *you* doing in that situation?" God may be revealing his kingdom in the midst of chaos, and bringing order and *shalom* to broken, hurting people. As the kingdoms of this world war against each other, you will begin to see the eternal kingdom as unshakeable, solid, and more beautiful than ever.

When missionaries were expelled from China in 1953, it would have been easy to see it as a major blow to the kingdom of heaven. But the Lord activated the Chinese brothers and sisters by removing the leaders who were preventing his movement from multiplying![10] What looked like a devastating blow to the kingdom ended up opening the door for the Holy Spirit to expand his work. When an earthquake or hurricane destroys an area, we naturally grieve; but we can also ask, "Spirit, comforter, who are you ministering to in eternally powerful ways through this? How can I participate in your work?" When one kingdom wars against another on this planet, we might say, "It looks dark from an earthly perspective, but what can the Holy Spirit do in his kingdom in spite of this?" While we still grieve and are heartbroken over the nature of such struggles, the expansion of the kingdom makes us ask new questions and look in new directions to find out what God is up to. Jesus said that the gates of hell will not prevail against his kingdom (Matthew 16:18).

Paradigm #4: APEST

APEST is the acronym for the five gifts shared in Ephesians 4—apostle, prophet, evangelist, shepherd, and teacher.

Before we dive into this paradigm, it is worth noting that in some circles, these gifts of the Holy Spirit have been abused. However, as

---

[10] A fascinating question here is, "What were the previous Christian leaders doing that was preventing multiplication? Why did it take their removal in order to trigger the epidemic expansion of the church in China?"

we have previously mentioned, abuse of a good thing doesn't warrant rejection of that good thing (as with food, sex, friendships, children, parents, etc.). Despite the unhealthy manifestations of these gifts in some circles, let us open our hearts to Scripture and how the Holy Spirit is leading us. The goal here is not to unpack the teachings of Ephesians 4, as they have been well explored elsewhere.[11] Study the Word for yourself to see whether these claims are true or false.

Solid scholarship argues that Ephesians was Paul's constitutional identity document for the church.[12] Forge America, The V3 Movement, and a growing number of missional networks, missions organizations, and denominations are discovering renewed vigor in the church by reflecting on Ephesians.[13] *The Permanent Revolution* by Alan Hirsch and Tim Catchim makes a strong and scholarly case for Ephesians as a key identity document for the church, and in our own study we have come to the same conclusions. Ephesians is addressed broadly and was expected to be circulated among various churches (as evidenced within the text). It seems clear that the book was not written because of an individual situation or a particular problem in a particular church, but rather that it was written to direct and deposit unique DNA into the churches. (This is unlike many of Paul's other epistles and letters.) An internal grammatical study of the book lends itself to this conclusion as well.

Just as a constitution provides guiding principles and a template for an organization or a people group's governance, Ephesians is written as a constitutional identity document for the church. We should therefore

---

[11] See Hirsch and Catchim, *The Permanent Revolution*; JR Woodward, *Creating a Missional Culture: Equipping the Church for the Sake of the World* (InterVarsity Press, 2012); and Woodward and White, *The Church as Movement*. Hirsch's main book on this topic is also well worth reading. See Alan Hirsch, *5Q: Reactivating the Original Intelligence and Capacity of the Body of Christ* (100 Movements Publishing, 2017).

[12] See N. T. Wright, *Paul for Everyone: The Prison Letters* (SPCK Publishing, 2002), 13; John Stott, *The Message of Ephesians: God's New Society*, 3rd ed. (InterVarsity Press, 1991), 14.

[13] See Russ Johnson and Tony Sorci, *Reclaim: Reclaiming the Church's Identity and Ministry as a Liberated People of Indiscriminate Grace* (Independently published, 2021) chapter 9, in the section titled "A Look at the Constitution in Ephesians 4:1–16."

pay attention to its special elements, as it contains several key passages with profound insight into the identity and DNA of the church. We would do well to read this book over and over, memorize it, and internalize it.

In looking at Ephesians, we see a beautiful outline emerge: Chapters 1–3 are oriented around solid, theological content, while chapters 4–6 are oriented around solid application and practical content. The flow of the book is part of its genius. Chapter 1 introduces a foundation of embodied Christology. (We are *in him*, which has amazing eternal and immediate implications for us.) Chapter 2 examines the beauty and impact of the salvation he has provided for us. Chapter 3 reminds us of the mysterious ways of the sovereignty of God, while culminating in one of the most beautiful and powerful prayers in all of Scripture.

Chapter 4 flows from our identity as a people *in him* (chapter 1), *empowered by him* (chapter 3), *enlivened by him* (chapter 2), etc. Chapter 4 builds upon this massive theological foundation with our identity being one in him as the global household of faith, and begins pointing to the uniqueness of this *one* faith, *one* love, *one* hope, etc., leading us to insights regarding spiritual gifts within the church. The purpose statement for these spiritual gifts—that the gifts exist for the equipping of the saints to do the work of ministry so that the body may be built up—leads us to understand how love and edification play out within the church.

Chapter 5 takes things a bit further into exhortations for almost every relational dynamic one might experience, showing how to live out the realities of the previous four chapters and linking marriage itself to the mysterious nature of Christ's love for the church. (We often note that marriage points to Christ, but then forget that according to Ephesians 5, it *also* points to the *church*! Incredible that the ideal of marriage parallels the ideal of the united *oneness* in the body of Christ. This is no surprise when you read Jesus' prayer in John 17.)

Chapter 6 reveals the nature of our struggle as being more than earthly, but reminds us that we are in a spiritual war between two universes. Chapter 6 also reveals the uniqueness of the spiritual tools available in Christ for us to put on by embracing the reality of being *in him* and living in a place of intercessory prayer.

All of this to say, we therefore find it strange that many have enjoyed the beauty and theological richness of *most* of Ephesians, while ignoring and/or writing off a significant portion of chapter 4. How can we take part of the chapter but not the whole? (We recognize that we have been guilty of this ourselves!)

Here is Ephesians 4:1–16.

> I therefore, a prisoner for the Lord, urge you to walk in a manner worthy of the calling to which you have been called, with all humility and gentleness, with patience, bearing with one another in love, eager to maintain the unity of the Spirit in the bond of peace. There is one body and one Spirit—just as you were called to the one hope that belongs to your call—one Lord, one faith, one baptism, one God and Father of all, who is over all and through all and in all. But grace was given to each one of us according to the measure of Christ's gift. Therefore it says,
>
> > "When he ascended on high he led a host of captives,
> > and he gave gifts to men."
>
> (In saying, "He ascended," what does it mean but that he had also descended into the lower regions, the earth? He who descended is the one who also ascended far above all the heavens, that he might fill all things.) And he gave the apostles, the prophets, the evangelists, the shepherds and teachers, to equip the saints for the work of ministry, for building up the body of Christ, until we all attain to the unity of the faith and of the knowledge of the Son of God, to mature manhood, to the measure of the stature of the fullness of Christ, so that we may no longer be children, tossed to and fro by the waves and carried about by every wind of doctrine, by human cunning, by craftiness in deceitful schemes. Rather, speaking the truth in love, we are to grow up in every way into him who is the head, into Christ, from whom the whole body, joined and held together by every joint

with which it is equipped, when each part is working properly, makes
the body grow so that it builds itself up in love.

There was a time in my (Jeremy's) life when it was easy for me to affirm
the first ten verses in this passage while making my own exegetical
gymnastics in order to ignore verse 11 ("And he gave the apostles,
the prophets, the evangelists, the shepherds and teachers). I would
immediately begin making side points and caveats about only two
of the gifts still operating (teacher and shepherd), while I ignored
or massively adjusted my definitions of the other three gifts. I was
blind to the fact that I was disregarding the whole in order to accept
the parts I found easier. But then, I began to see things in the text
differently, and to understand the importance of affirming the *entire*
chapter. In the past, I would walk people through a grammatical
layout of Ephesians (in the Greek) and demonstrate just how we
could put verse 11 away, appealing to the "whole of Scripture" as a
means to do so. But while overseas, I began to see the Lord working
in ways that implied something different about this passage. I also
began to see insights about how the body of Christ works together
as a team.

Notice how the passage mentions all this "oneness" (one body, one
Spirit, one hope, etc.). Paul is laying the groundwork for understanding
the unity and diversity within the body of Christ. In verse 7 he explains
that God has given grace to *each one* (implying *every single believer!*)
according to the measure of Christ's gift. Then in verse 11, he unpacks
what that grace (given to each believer) looks like.

Here, we will break verses 11 and 12 down:

**Verses 11–12—"And he gave the apostles, the prophets, the
evangelists, the shepherds, and teachers, *to equip*":** This is a purpose
statement, and none of the other passages about gifts—1 Corinthians
12, Romans 12, 1 Peter 4—give such a statement. We would do well to
consider the importance/benefit of attaching a purpose statement to
spiritual gifts.

Verse 12—"the saints *for the work of ministry*": This clarifies
further the purpose of these gifts (and those who have these gifts): to

resource, give tools, and prepare the holy people of God to do the work of servanthood.

Verse 12—*"for the building up* of the body of Christ": Additional clarification to that purpose statement: These gifts exist *so that* the body may be built up.

Hmm … do you think the body no longer needs these gifts or that the body no longer needs to be built up? Clearly, there is still a need for saints to be equipped to do the work of servanthood so that the church of Jesus Christ can be built up more and more.

If we go back and look at verses 13–16, the end result is unity (which Paul was speaking about in verses 1–10), maturity, and love.

The logical argument being made is this: There is one body of Christ and one faith. This faith/body is built up as a result of the gift of grace given by Jesus through the five gifts that are mentioned. The logic is clear.

So, let's unpack these five gifts: apostle, prophet, evangelist, shepherd, and teacher. The following definitions are used globally but are also linked to extensive study of their grammatical contexts and usage within Scripture as well as extra-canonical usage.

If you struggle with the term "gift" or the APEST terms themselves, consider them as personality types. What would these personality types do for the benefit of the body? Even if you erase them as gifts, you must be able to acknowledge that the body of Christ would benefit from people having a variety of particular skills and personalities oriented toward the good of the whole. Some individuals have also spoken of these orientations as "five voices" in the business world.[14]

- **Apostle:** One who is sent. A pioneer. One who takes new ground and is especially concerned with igniting those things that result in the multiplication of the body of Christ. Think of these people as Spirit-empowered, pioneering entrepreneurs, or the ones who are obsessed with breaking the mold or expanding or starting brand-new systems.

---

[14] See https://5voices.com/.

- **Prophet:** Those who concern themselves with justice, living out the application of truth, confronting darkness, pointing people back to the heart of God and the purity of holiness. These are the people who challenge systems, urge the culture toward change, and desire to set people free. They are activists.
- **Evangelist:** Those who speak the good news. They love stories and see them as transformative. They see the wisdom intrinsic to storytelling. They are contagious. They easily convince others and invite people in. These are the people who have great relational insight to help win people over to their side. In the workplace, these are often recruiters and salespeople.
- **Shepherd:** These are the relational glue. They care for souls and have insight into how to show love, kindness, hospitality, and how to build community. This gift helps the body stay together as the body! These people are caregivers, people who delight in helping others to grow, heal, recover, and improve. They counsel others and help others feel loved.
- **Teacher:** These are not just educators but philosophical types, people who speak about "truth." They are concerned with helping others grow in knowledge, awareness, and perspective. Teachers love to make lists and outlines to help move appropriate data into structures that are accessible to others.

Paradigm #5: Jesus-Shaped APEST

Which was Jesus? All of them! he was the perfect representation of the fivefold gifts. Jesus was the ultimate forerunner of all apostles— he pioneered into this world to pave the way for an eternal kingdom. Jesus was the ultimate prophet—most people even mistook him for Elijah. He spoke to the injustice of the system; he flipped tables because people were greedy instead of prayerful; he cared more about the heart of God than anyone ever has; he came to set captives free. Jesus was the ultimate evangelist, preaching the good news of the kingdom, of love, of life, of being born again, of the water of life, of the Holy Spirit, etc. Jesus was the ultimate Shepherd—he even said about himself, "I am the Good Shepherd." He cared for the hurting and sick; he brought healing; he cared for children and women (which was countercultural for such an "important male" in first-century Middle Eastern culture). Jesus was the ultimate teacher, constantly communicating truth and creating environments for learning, urging the disciples toward truth in all things.

Paradigm #6: APEST Imbalances

Each of these gifts can also lead to imbalances. Apostles may break off from community to start something new, "running over" other people en route to the next new thing. Prophets may challenge without mercy, self-control, care, diplomacy, or patience. Evangelists may be too eager and spread themselves too thin. They can easily manipulate people because of their power to convince others. Shepherds can slow things down by *not* being willing to sacrifice for the sake of the wider movement; they can be too inward-focused and lose perspective of the broader work of God. Teachers may be good at *talking* and lack in doing or being. They may speak too long or act like "know-it-alls."

Every gift passage in Scripture comes with a beautiful deposit when read in context: love. Look for yourself. *No* passage in Scripture that discusses gifts is without mention of love. Love will guide the gifts; and when we allow the Holy Spirit his place in our lives, we will avoid these immature uses of the gifts. If we neglect love, then the intelligence and skills of each gift can become toxic and destructive to the body.

Let the fruits of the Spirit direct the gifts of the Spirit!

Paradigm #7: APEST Hermeneutics

How you see the world with these gifts will influence how you interpret Scripture. Postmodern theory promotes humility in our interpretations—it helps us understand that the mental grids or lenses that we each possess can sometimes skew our individual interpretation of Scripture.

Take John 3:16, for example. It is possible to preach five different sermons on this passage depending on *your* particular APEST gift:

Apostles emphasize that God so loved the world that he *sent* his Son. It is the *mission* of God into this world that reflects our missionary God! Apostles get animated about this point.

Prophets emphasize the difference between "believe" and *really* believing by *acting* upon that belief. A prophet would also be attentive to the beautiful and eternally poetic sacrifice God made in sending his *only* begotten Son and what that meant to a Trinity in perfect unity.

Evangelists consider this verse to mean that *life* and salvation are available to all who believe. This is *great news!*

Shepherds are quick to notice the *love* that God has for the world and that God is willing to protect anyone who believes from perishing by providing everlasting life.

Teachers emphasize what it means to actually believe this truth. They would also do what I (Jeremy) just did in this section by laying out so many details. Teachers will want to write another book about APEST hermeneutics. (*Oh, I would love to do that! I actually started a manuscript a few years ago on this topic. Maybe I should get on that …!*)

Paradigm #8: The Homeless Man and APEST

One further illustration. A team of an apostle, a prophet, an evangelist, a shepherd, and a teacher walk into a bar. As they arrive, they notice a drunk, homeless man walking out of the bar. Suddenly, he falls and strikes his knee on the ground. He is bleeding.

The *apostle* says, "We must serve this man, for through him, his friends and social circles may be impacted by the gospel. Perhaps if he begins walking with Jesus, many homeless people will be freed and come to know God's love!"

The *prophet* says, "We must exhort this man to stop drinking in excess and to press toward holiness in all areas of his life. We must challenge him to begin finding his way back toward the dignity of work!"

The *teacher* looks at the apostle and prophet with an odd expression on his face and says, "Sure, we can do that. But first, we'll need to teach him how to get back on his feet since he clearly hasn't had any appropriate instruction."

The *shepherd* pipes up, "Guys, you can do all that, but this guy just needs a Band-Aid and a hug right now! Perhaps later, as we develop a friendship with him, we can help find him a home and a job."

Then the *evangelist* (who has already had a drink with a friend at the bar) comes over, and laughs, and says (a little too loudly), "GUYS … no, no, no! ALL HE NEEDS IS JESUS!"

But then Love walks into the bar and says, "You are all wrong, and you are all right. But do not forget: Love this man … *because* … *love*."

Paradigm #9: APEST and Other Spiritual Gifts

APEST isn't as rigid as every individual having one gift and none of the others. As we see in Jesus, all five of the gifts are perfectly present. Each person has been given a mix of giftings but may have particular strengths in one or two areas. Gifts can layer within individuals with beautiful, infinite diversity. Imagine how an apostolic-prophet would be compared to an apostolic-shepherd? Imagine a shepherding-teacher compared to a shepherding-evangelist.

We can go further with this thought. Look at how a person who is gifted in giving will function based on APEST: An apostolic-giver might intentionally fund church planting and missions; a shepherding-giver might fund soul-care ministries; a teaching-giver might fund a seminary scholarship, etc.

This can also be seen with the spiritual gift of hospitality or the gift of administration. Each of these gifts, along with APEST, can look different depending on how the gifts influence each other. Now take it further by considering how these gifts would impact the lists of gifts in 1 Corinthians 12 and Romans 12.

Some people also switch or toggle from one gift to another. Catchim and Hirsch, in their lectures, refer to this as "base and phase," where you have a base gift, which is your default operational mode, and a phase gift, which you press into when you see the seasonal or contextual need for it. Sometimes an entire season of life will require you to use a phase gift that you wouldn't otherwise have naturally gravitated toward. This becomes clearer when you are on the forefront of kingdom expansion. When you take new territory for Christ, you may suddenly find that there are *no* shepherds around, but the need for shepherding is *huge*, so you will step into the role of shepherd out of love and a desire to see health in those you are ministering to. There are further APEST dynamics at work when we consider the particular cultures of our families, workplaces, church environments, and even our countries. (What country has more salespeople—evangelist orientation—than the US? Or consider how some cultures are more didactic/teaching-oriented than others.) Denominations and networks can take on particular qualities of the APEST gifts. Being aware of this diversity of gifts can help you notice gaps, appreciate others, love them, and be grateful for the diversity that exists within the body.

Paradigm #10: Polycentric Leadership

When we look at 1 Peter 2:9, we see that we are a royal priesthood. All believers make up this priesthood. If we take this seriously, it would follow that there is some level of significant involvement for every single one of us. It would logically follow that the Almighty King wants all of us to play a particular role in this world. *This has significant implications for our approach to leadership structures.* Jesus calls us the salt of the earth (Matthew 5:19) and the light of the world (Matthew 5:14). This implies that we *all* can play a role in being preserving agents in this world and in carrying forth his message to others. Jesus' commission also implies this, "Go into all the world and *make disciples*" (Matthew 28:19, emphasis ours). We go, and wherever we go, we draw people into the apprenticeship of Jesus, that they may learn to follow his ways and be immersed in the "Trinitarian reality."[15] We can look at APEST and come to the same conclusion: If the Lord has given certain gifts *for the purpose* of equipping the saints to do the work of servanthood

---

[15] We have often heard Dallas Willard say this in his lectures.

so that the body can be built up and mature, then we should especially cultivate the awareness and practice of these gifts and prioritize those who are mature in the use of these gifts (a key principle here) to speak into our leadership culture in our organizations and gatherings.

If you take this approach, then the Scriptures that talk about elders and deacons also become more intuitive. Leadership will become more of a team approach rather than a top-down or hierarchical system; it will become polycentric (centered on the team and the gifts of the team) rather than centralized.

Polycentric is a better word than "decentralized" because, as Woodward and White point out in *The Church as Movement*, decentralized can sometimes create chaos and inactivity due to group paralysis. There always needs to be those who step up and initiate, strategize, influence, and call others forward, so there is still a clear need for leadership; but polycentric leadership matches more intuitively with the biblical doctrines of the priesthood of all believers, eldership/deaconship, and especially APEST.

Polycentric leadership allows multiple voices to speak into decisions while still allowing for the simplicity of a few individuals taking initiative. As we have seen, not everyone actually wants to participate in certain decisions; it is an act of servanthood to *sometimes* allow a few to make the decision for the whole. It is also true that many are so weighed down with their own lives or the inability to make healthy decisions for themselves that they might say, "Please, go ahead and make the call. I don't have capacity to figure these things out." It is in this way that polycentric leadership initiatives are an act of servanthood to the entire group. "Decision fatigue" is real and continues to grow. Despite the idealistic purity of some who advocate for reaching perfect consensus,[16] there needs to be room for groups to move quickly rather than requiring the entire group to hash out every single detail of smaller decisions. Creating and developing APEST teams is an excellent polycentric option.

---

[16] Frank Viola's literature particular frames group leadership in this way. See Frank Viola, *Reimagining Church: Pursuing the Dream of Organic Christianity* (David C. Cook, 2008).

Notice the language we use here: We are not condemning other leadership structures. We understand that there are situations where it is fine to even have one leader "calling the shots" for a time and that allowing one person to be the "tie breaker" seems quite rational and beneficial in order for organizations to function. However, we are proposing that polycentric leadership allows teams to multiply faster and in healthier ways. It has been our experience in both the US and globally that polycentric leadership structures enable a team of elders who recognize their APEST gifting to develop leaders who are well-equipped to identify and raise up new leaders without any one leader being bogged down.[17]

A quick word on "leadership." The New Testament doesn't use the word "leader" very often. It talks more about gifting or elders; and even then, Jesus, when speaking on leadership, warned us *not* to be like those who lead in the world—those who rule for selfish ambition and self-promotion. Instead, he called us to serve and sacrifice our lives for others.

True leadership is a call to pain and suffering (look at the cross!), a call to humiliation (again, look at the cross!), and a call to personal sacrifice for the good of others. Leadership does not put itself first but must be an act and demeanor of love. True leadership requires the integrity of character to be self-forgetful, others-mindful, Christ-obsessed and kingdom-oriented.

Crawford Loritts, in his classic *Leadership as an Identity*, makes a case for leadership that is birthed from deep calling, a deep desire to serve, and the character that is formed through loss, suffering, failure, and humiliation.[18] Leadership convergence happens when someone is committed to doing what is right, doing it in the right way, and for the right motives. Loritts proposes that instead of needing books on leadership, we need more books on character. He says that one of

---

[17] If you are interested in continuing this conversation, we can't recommend enough Woodward and White's *The Church as Movement*; Woodward's *Creating a Missional Culture*; Hirsch's *The Forgotten Ways* and *5Q*; Hirsch and Catchim's *The Permanent Revolution*; Alan Roxburgh's *Missional*; and Hugh Halter's writings.

[18] Loritts, *Leadership as an Identity*.

the worst things we can do to a young person is tell them, "You are going to be a leader someday!" (In doing this, we set them up to have a vision *of themselves* being something impressive, but the vision is of themselves, not of the people they are serving). Instead, we should tell young people, "Focus on growth in Christ, on character, on intimacy with Jesus, and one day you will serve and sacrifice for others in untold ways, for his glory." Imagine the difference it would make if we thought about leadership in this way.

When we say "polycentric leadership," we mean "polycentric sacrifice, humility, and servanthood." We envision equippers of others who work as a team to see the cause of Christ advance in this world.

Paradigm #11: Multiplication of Midwives

Our role is like that of a midwife.[19] A midwife is present to oversee a birth—new life emerging. When the birthing process is happening, the focus is *not* on the midwife; the focus is on the child *and* on the mother. The focus is urgent. The goal is the healthy perpetuation of life. No one asks how the midwife is feeling or what perspective the midwife has on these things. The midwife is engaged in the urgency of helping things along. Birth will happen with or without the midwife— the midwife just exists to help the process. Since birth is rather messy, a midwife helps to take care of that mess. The midwife participates in the joy of the day, but it is not about the midwife.

We may do well to replace the word "leadership" with "servants" ("midwives" works too—we have heard of some groups use this language). But rather than legalistically forcing a change of wording, let us lean into embodying this new language, enticing ourselves with the beauty of humility that comes from being *servants* rather than *leaders*.

Movement wisdom also requires multiplication at every level. In APEST, multiplication makes a *lot* of sense. If we follow Jesus' model,

---

[19] Michael Frost and Christina Rice also use this terminology of "midwives" with respect to ministry in their book *To Alter Your World*. Michael Frost and Christina Rice, *To Alter Your World: Partnering with God to Rebirth Our Communities* (InterVarsity Press, 2017).

people will be constantly learning to create a culture of apprenticeship, helping identify the gifts and roles that will be best for others to walk in, and then raising them up in these things. (This will happen when an APEST team works in maturity.) Movement wisdom requires that our teams split or *send*. Sending is healthier for teams than splitting. It is typically less emotionally difficult for the group, especially for the shepherds, if we identify those we will *send* instead of just ripping a team apart.[20]

This work of multiplication is only successful when initiating servants step into the role of actually leading new groups. Usually, in church-planting movements or epidemic discipleship phenomenon, this new leadership happens organically (naturally) and in an intuitive way. It's like there is a collective genius at work in the body where it just makes sense that this particular person with a certain passion, a demonstrated willingness to serve, and a direction or orientation of movement is blessed and sanctified to go forth and make disciples in a new context.

Paradigm #12: It's Easier than You Think

It can be difficult to see multiplication on a macro level. Some organizations talk about the multiplication of churches, but Jesus *never* told his followers to multiply churches. He said, "Make disciples." Jesus gave us parables of multiplication at work. He trained three and twelve disciples, and it appears that the Twelve would have led the Seventy-Two when Jesus sent them out (see Luke 9–11). We see that Jesus has led his kingdom toward multiplication through the ages. But let's keep this in tension with the other thing Jesus said—that the gate is narrow and few will find the road (Matthew 7:13–14). Jesus also said that many will be called, but the chosen are few. Yet much is written in Scripture about triumph, victory, and the gates of hell *not* prevailing against his church. These tensions allow us to walk in humility. When

---

[20] This being the case, it can still feel like a loss when we send a beloved friend out on mission. In Acts 20:36–37, we see the believers grieving when Paul moves on to the next stage of mission.

we talk about multiplication, we should orient ourselves first toward the multiplication that comes from making followers of Jesus and helping them make followers of Jesus. This is where it gets simple.

Making a disciple may be as simple as coming alongside someone and helping them learn to talk to Jesus, walk in the Spirit by learning to listen, and begin reading the Gospels so that they can see and experience Jesus firsthand. It's about helping them to ask questions about who he was and is, what he did and why he did it, then assisting them to obey in grace. It sounds too simple, but it really is that simple. We are the ones who complexify it (and yes, that is a word)! The simplicity of the task is why some movements have expanded so well.[21]

Let's not forget that our leader, our King, our ultimate role model, Jesus himself violated *many* of our discipleship books and processes when he told the former Gerasene demoniac to go back to his town and tell people what Jesus had done for him (Mark 5:18–20). The guy was basically pleading with Jesus to allow him to follow him, yet Jesus denied him!

Imagine Jesus, of all people, saying, "No, don't come and learn from me. Instead, go and become a missionary to the cities you came from." This tells us that Jesus was operating with great spiritual insight and wisdom. He saw what the Father was doing and urged the man to go and participate in what the Father was about to do.

The Ethiopian eunuch (Acts 8:26–40) is another excellent example of the Spirit of God violating all of our modern discipleship programs. The eunuch is saved, and then Phillip is transported away before he can begin to disciple this new believer. The eunuch only had a small amount of scriptural literature, the knowledge of Christ, and the indwelling Holy Spirit, which apparently was enough. One can also safely assume that at Pentecost, when three thousand were added to the disciples' number (Acts 2:41), many of those people had come from numerous nations and would leave within days. No discipleship program went with them, but the Spirit of God did. Making disciples is

---

[21] See, for example, the movements studied by David Garrison in his literature, Steve Addison, and other church-planting movements in India, Peru, etc.

not as difficult as we make it out to be sometimes, even though it may require sacrifices that feel difficult. This tension between rapid reproduction and faithful depth allows us to grow in maturity as we learn to discern the work the Lord is inviting us into.

Paradigm #13: Cities

Notice how both Jesus and Paul focused on cities. (Looking at the theme of "cities" throughout Scripture can make for a great study.)[22] Cities impact regions. Even today, global movement toward urbanization is significant.[23] Ralph Winter, the famous missiologist, stated decades ago that the future of missions was in the cities, and he clearly wasn't wrong.[24] Jeremy recalls his first time flying over Sao Paulo, Brazil, and seeing the massive city stretched out below for miles. It was his first time there, and the miles of houses and people seemed never-ending. As he looked down, his soul interceded for a movement of God in that city.

Cities concentrate creativity, increase the speed of synergy between people groups, amplify the cross-pollination of ideas from divergent disciplines, and maximize human potential. Cities are places of culture creation and dissemination of new ideas, art, culture, and movements.

The internet has also created a global urbanizing effect. People in rural areas are being exposed to pluralistic and global ideas and cultural influences. We can fear these realities—perhaps aware of the many dark aspects of the internet and its influence—or we can embrace the opportunities to spread the kingdom of light to reach all the peoples of the earth. We need to innovate and adapt when looking into ministries of online presence. We have personally participated in online missionary programs and seen firsthand the beauty of reaching the nations from home via technology. Global Media Outreach is a

---

[22] Timothy Keller discusses this brilliantly in *Center Church*.

[23] "Urbanization," https://ourworldindata.org/urbanization.

[24] Ralph Winter, "The High Priority: Cross-Cultural Evangelism," *Perspectives on the World Christian Movement*, 4th ed. (William Carey Publishing, 2009).

prime example. Jeremy worked with them as an online missionary for a number of years and saw fruit every day. In recent years, we have seen and experimented with numerous missional endeavors on dozens of online platforms that have enabled a faithful witness to reach many people.

We have a friend who video chats with strangers on various websites and has found herself sharing Jesus with people around the world, every day. Many times, people break down in tears saying that it was an answer to their prayers or that they were suicidal that morning and she happened to be the catalyst that reminded them of the love of God, so they end up putting confidence in Jesus! We have several friends who participate in online gaming communities and build friendships that allow them to speak the gospel fluently and effectively into the pain and brokenness of those around them. Others are creatively building content for the purpose of spreading the seeds of the good news in those online environments. How might the Lord use your creative abilities for his movement?

MOVEMENT WISDOM TOOLS

Tools are the adaptable, practical methods that light our way. Like a handheld torch, tools illuminate specific areas of need or challenge, guiding our actions. Not every practice will be suitable for every situation. Therefore, careful discernment is crucial in selecting the right tool for the task. Once a particular tool effectively reveals solutions, we can apply it with increasing diligence and frequency, focusing our efforts where they are most needed.

Tool #1: Kingdom Prayer and 24-Hour Prayer

If we look at the movement of God from a kingdom-of-heaven perspective, we find that prayer is a vital component of kingdom movement. Out of the many communities we have helped to birth, not *one single* community started without intensive prayer. Sometimes it was just two of us in a room praying weekly for a few months before anything took shape. In their book *Red Moon Rising*, Pete Grieg and

Dave Roberts mention the history of the 24/7 prayer movements that spread across Europe and eventually went global.[25] After reading the book and visiting a 24/7 prayer room, we were inspired by the reality that we must be a people who pray. So, we took the joy upon ourselves to do 24 hours of prayer. The results were incredible. It awakened a deeper sense of who God is, who we are as the family of God, and what the Lord cares about in his movement. Imagine the impact if more people would even host just one 24–hour prayer vigil per year in their city (let alone the intense pursuit of creating ongoing prayer rooms for unceasing prayer)!

Tool #2: APEST Hats

Alan Hirsch recommends that teams learn to think through the APEST gift orientations. If a team analyzes a particular issue they are facing and considers how each of the APEST giftings would approach it, they can form a more holistic and thorough response. To illustrate, using the earlier example of APEST and the homeless man at the bar on pages 109–110, the team might collectively ask, "Okay, let's put on the apostle hat for a moment. What would the apostle do?" Suddenly, people in the team would see things differently and become more open to new possibilities and opportunities that their gifting may have blinded them to. The team could then repeat this for each of the other "hats," ensuring they don't neglect any of the other APEST giftings.

Tool #3: The 5 Cs

It is common in leadership studies to cite the 5 Cs: *character*, *chemistry*, *capacity*, *calling*, and *competence*. These are five qualities you can look for when identifying a potential apprentice or a new addition to your team.

---

[25] Pete Grieg and Dave Roberts, *Red Moon Rising: Rediscover the Power of Prayer* (David C. Cook, 2015).

You will want someone who has *character* (trustworthy, full of goodness, and overflowing with the ways of life and the Spirit of life).

You will also look for some level of *chemistry* with you and the rest of the team. This means compatibility at some level, although people of character can learn to create this among themselves. Still, you want the chemistry to reflect common values, common practices, common theology, and common vision. Otherwise, you may not be the best fit to work together in a team. If there is no chemistry, it might be better to remain associates in the same city or region and partner together on larger-scale endeavors, but continue in separate teams for the most part.

Capacity is vital. You may find someone with the other four elements who just doesn't have the time, energy, or resources to partner with you in a faithful, dependable, and trustworthy manner. Capacity changes over time. For example, a single man in your team may have significant capacity to help with a missional community, but when he gets married and starts a family, he has different priorities and therefore different capacity. Someone else in our team might suddenly have an estate to deal with or a dying parent, or they develop chronic pain that reduces their capacity. As capacity changes, we must adapt. We must reproduce our roles quickly to avoid the waxing and waning of our team's capacity to hinder progress.

Calling is the notion that someone is truly walking in the direction that the Lord is leading them. You don't want someone to be in a role they were not intended or prepared for. But, to be disciples of Jesus means that we will often be placed in situations or roles that will challenge our strengths. Jesus sometimes asks a non-teacher to teach, an unmerciful person to be merciful, a non-evangelist to share good news, a non-giver to give anyway. We can't use our lack of gifting in this area to call us away from obedience; yet we must still be attentive to the roles that make the most sense given the underlying temperament and skillset that the Holy Spirit has given us.

Competence is the ability to do our assignments well. Some people are competent in working with children, while others are more competent in teaching adults. Being attentive to someone's ability to handle the mantle of responsibility placed on them is a way of shepherding them and lovingly putting them in roles that stretch but don't crush them.

With each of these five Cs, surprises lurk around every corner! In our experience, it takes a year minimum to identify if these qualities are truly present in someone's life. (Some people say it takes even two years!) Therefore, if we are going to be responsible in multiplying servant leaders, it may take a lot longer than we had hoped. Patience is a supreme virtue in these processes.

Tool #4: MAWLR

Another helpful tool is: Model, Assist, Watch, Launch, Repeat (MAWLR). This helps us to think about the process of training and apprenticing others.

Take the disciple-making role or the servanthood or initiating role that you are currently doing and *model* it to someone for a period of time. Have them *assist* you in accomplishing tasks (start small), then *watch* them as they begin to lead, then *launch* them into action on their own. Finally, *repeat* it and have them *repeat* it. Otherwise, you will only see addition instead of multiplication. They must be aware that they are going through the MAWLR process so that they can repeat it with someone else.

Tool #5: WORST Peer Coaching

Another useful tool for helping one another develop as leaders is peer coaching. Movements will spread when we work together in interdependence to help one another succeed. WORST coaching is something we developed for this purpose:

- **Wins:** What are the recent goals they have achieved? (Start the conversation in a positive direction.)
- **Obstacles:** What are some hindrances to their current goals (areas to overcome)?

- **Resources:** What are some vitally helpful resources for this person?
- **Solutions:** Are there any immediate and obvious solutions to identify?
- **Timeline:** When will they act upon the steps identified in this process?

Tool #6: Contextualization and Discernment

Because it is vital in shaping your thinking about movement, let's quickly look at Tool #1 from chapter three again. We can use this tool to analyze the culture of your team (as well as the wider culture). Are you working with movement-oriented wisdom in your team culture?

- **Linguistic insight:** What does the language of this missional community reveal? Is it sensitive to God's global movement and stewardship of multiplication?
- **Cultural texts or artifacts:** What tools do we have to use, and how do they shape us as a community? Do they represent an awareness and intelligence of movement? Or are our artifacts too unsustainable or unreproducible? A great example of this is a former global evangelistic movement that Jeremy was connected to. They created a complex but fascinating tool that had to be mass-produced and shipped out in order to be used in evangelism; but in doing so, they also created a culture where individuals wouldn't share their faith unless they had the tool with them. This meant that people really struggled to multiply, and others would say, "I would like to share my faith, but first I have to get a tool like yours!" The tool (artifact) was preventing true freedom in the movement. Eventually they shifted to a different, more reproducible tool, which was a move toward maturity for that organization.
- **Beliefs:** What are the faith assumptions and values that shape our decisions and actions? E.g., do we actually share an assumption that God values multiplication?
- **Causes:** What is God calling us to do? Do we believe that his

mission involves epidemic growth elements? Do we trust the Holy Spirit to guide the movement?

- **Measurements:** What does it mean to be faithful and fruitful in God's mission? Do we celebrate the tiniest bit of faithful reproduction?
- **Rituals and methodologies:** What are the core practices we are engaging in? Are they easily reproducible? Are they memorable? Are they sticky? *Or* are they complex, unwieldy, heavy, and unsustainable for people? (Do they mobilize the priesthood of believers or not?)
- **Plans:** How will we fulfill God's calling together? Are we using wisdom and listening to the Spirit of God? (These are one and the same—true wisdom is always of the Spirit of God).

Tool #7: Personal Multiplication Axiom: 3, 2, 1

A personal multiplication axiom that we use is 3, 2, 1. We can aim to be spiritually forming with three people, reaching out evangelistically toward two, and apprenticing one.[26] If you are spiritually growing with three, then you have a tiny gathering of believers; if each of you is reaching two, then you have a missional community and a clearly directed context of outreach; and if you are each apprenticing at least one other person, then you will naturally be multiplying.

Tool #8: People of Peace as Movement Wisdom

In chapter three, we considered people of peace and mentioned Malcolm Gladwell's insights from *The Tipping Point*. People of peace

---

[26] Spiritually forming means growing deeply in the formative practices of following Jesus, allowing his Spirit to be shaping our hearts, minds, and souls. Evangelistically reaching out means intentionally seeking opportunities to be spreading good news into the lives of others, intentionally waiting to see when someone is at a place where the Spirit of God can use us to help them make necessary shifts in their lives. Apprenticing is essentially introducing someone to the patterns and practices we follow so that they might imitate us as we imitate Christ.

and people who open doors for the gospel to go forth are connectors, mavens (people of massive information), and salespeople or persuaders. For the sake of movement, we need more followers of Jesus to think in terms of being an epidemic of faith that spreads around the world. Minister, love, and serve those in your life who are connectors. Let them see Jesus shining gloriously and lovingly through your life.

Pay particular attention to those who are magnets for information. In this information age, people need those who have wisdom, not just knowledge. Go to those information junkies and help them see how to move beyond information to transformation. This shift will bless them. Once a person stops gaining information for information's sake and starts looking for transformation, their life will be drastically altered.

Our culture often undervalues or misunderstands the role of salespeople and persuaders. They may have exceptional people skills, yet they are often used and alone. Let us intentionally love these people.

There is a tension here between macro and micro perspectives. Don't think about the individual without thinking about the movement, but don't think about the movement without thinking about the individual. If you treat people as stepping stones toward some "movement achievement," you will never see true fruit, and people will get hurt. But if you neglect the wider movement of God, then you will lose perspective even with the individuals you are ministering to. We need this macro/micro tension in our discipleship and in our movement thinking.

If we focus on people without considering the movement of God, then we *neglect his heart* as it beats for the nations. If we focus on the movement without loving people, then we *sabotage both*.

IT'S SCRIPTURAL. IT'S RATIONAL. IT'S TRANSFORMATIONAL.

We have seen that these practices are biblical. It is the blessing of God that allows us to be fruitful and multiply (not just in biological procreation but in spiritual procreation). It is the product of the kingdom of heaven being spread forth by the power of the Holy Spirit. To deny these truths would require turning a blind eye to many scriptural texts.

But beyond that, these tools are rational and simple! They have been tested and demonstrated in the secular world, but more importantly, they have been tested and demonstrated to be transformational in the spiritual realm. We have seen lives impacted globally by applying the practices and tools in this chapter.

5

ORGANIC SYSTEMS
Structuring for Multiplication

 KEY IDEAS

- When we say, "It's simpler than you think," we aren't kidding!
- God has made us to be relational beings. His ways and principles integrate perfectly with the relational dynamics he has put within us.
- Our systems teach us much more than we realize.
- Our systems can either kill the movement or enable and free all believers to play significant roles in the kingdom of heaven.
- Non-organic is hard to multiply and unsustainable in the long-term, but organic multiplies faster than you can imagine. We must lay aside our desire for "control" and release the body to be the body.

SEE FOR YOURSELF

Read Acts and ask yourself: What does this show about the structures and systems the early church used? In what ways are we living "the church" out today in a similar way to the early church? How could we do so more?

To go further, read Luke, and write down your observations about the relational structures that seemed sufficient to Jesus.

ORGANIC SYSTEMS FOUNDATIONS

Foundations are our unshakable core map, charting the terrain. Foundations provide the rock-solid theological principles that remain constant, regardless of the specific location or context we find ourselves in. They equip and prepare us for the journey, ensuring we have a reliable understanding of the fundamental landscape.

Foundation #1: High Relational Integrity and Commitment

In *The Forgotten Ways*, Alan Hirsch describes how "organic systems" are integral to movements. Organic systems have naturally occurring social patterns and behaviors that lend themselves toward expansive, movement-oriented, contagious social epidemics. If something is natural and intuitive (i.e., it's not manufactured or high maintenance), it can be quickly passed on to others. Hirsch also says that "phenomenal Jesus movements grow precisely because they do not have centralized institutions to block growth through control.... Remarkable Jesus movements have the feel of a movement, structure as a network, and spread like viruses."[1] Church as an industrial complex, corporation, or enterprise is not as easy to reproduce as spontaneous gatherings of disciples. We recognize the beauty and function that more established church structures have in the global body of Christ, yet, it's also important to highlight the option of church as organic, simple gatherings. These can sometimes be impromptu and Spirit-led and other times more intentional and structured. But either way, these gatherings are naturally occurring as a product of relationships and spiritual friendships.

Organic is natural. However, organic is not necessarily the "easier

---

[1] Hirsch, *The Forgotten Ways*, 25.

way" of church. When "church" exists as a Sunday service where one can slip in and out without any accountability or commitment to relationships, it might be seen as easier than organic forms of church. The substance of organic church is the people who are part of it and their collective identity. To be the kind of church Jesus called us to be requires covenantal love toward one another—arguably harder and messier than more structured forms of church.

In organic church settings, there is a high threshold of responsibility placed on each person, particularly if they are willing to press into deeper relationship with one another and embody the kind of discipleship we see in the Gospels and early church. Conversely, consumer-oriented religious goods and services are sometimes misleading in terms of the true cost of discipleship. They can also be difficult to reproduce as they require a huge amount of resources and "professional" leadership.

Organic church shouldn't be without a system, though. It isn't simply a "go with the flow" approach with no structure. Organic systems are a sort of trellis, providing the structure of the ecclesial architecture to mobilize God's global movement. It's important not to criticize the structures of other churches or models or deconstruct without providing a new construct. Everywhere we have personally experienced organic church—in tribal India, the sand dunes of Africa, a cidery in Richmond, a labyrinth in Ireland, an online call, a canyon near Denver, a marketplace in Sweden, and in the Andes Mountains of Peru and Chile —the commitment has been one of high relational integrity.

Foundation #2: Our Systems Shape Us

We shape our buildings, then they shape us. Sometimes the easiest way to block certain values is to shape our social constructs accordingly. For example, if you want to have higher group participation in a classroom, put the chairs in a circle; but if you want the class to focus on only one individual, keep the chairs in rows facing the teacher's podium. You shape your constructs to facilitate the nourishment of your values.

Some cultures have homes that are round to create a centering circle within the family. In contrast, other cultures have homes full of right angles, reflecting certain values of efficiency regarding the placement of objects within the home. Neither is better than the other. They are just oriented differently for different purposes and values.

Some church systems are structured to tell people that there are only a few professional religious leaders in the congregation; other church systems are oriented to tell people that the leader is a celebrity; others have set up systems that reflect the importance of certain spiritual disciplines (stations of the cross in a cathedral, for example); meanwhile, other systems are intended to encourage various forms of worship. The list could go on. This can extend from the physical shapes and set-up of our buildings to our social structures and ways we meet—our small groups, or Sunday school groups, how we arrange our monthly and annual rhythms as a church, etc.

Most of us don't really notice our structures and their effect on shaping us. But our structures can teach us more than many sermons combined. They speak louder than words and sometimes louder than actions—teaching and imparting invisible values. We should consider our current structures and what they impart to us. But we can also find ways to shape our structures and systems to be more organic, in order to harness the power of kingdom multiplication. As we will see, lowering the structural threshold can be massively empowering to the priesthood of all believers.

Foundation #3: Even a Single Cell Organism Has Structure

Structure can be arranged with simplicity for the purpose of profundity. Simple structure can look like creating a monthly rhythm for your group, focused around In, Out, Up, and Beyond: *In* (ministry to the followers of Jesus in a group), *Out* (ministry toward others), *Up* (worshipful intimacy with the Lord), *Beyond* (strategic brainstorming and self-governing of the group). A group can increase and decrease its gathering frequency as needed. Some groups may find opportunities to meet multiple times in one week and then take a month off, while others may only meet monthly. We have seen a dramatic range in missional rhythms and structures.

Eradicating all structure creates anarchy or paralysis, while maintaining some degree of rhythm and leadership produces an intentional disciple-making environment, in which we lend ourselves and our structures to the working of the Holy Spirit. Depending on the size of the group, leadership can be multiplied simply and organically (relationally). In smaller groups (2–8 people), it may make the most sense to have just one initiator/director for the group, while in larger groups (8+ people), it makes sense to create a team approach to leadership. (APEST helps to identify various roles that this polycentric leadership structure can fall into.) Many missional practitioners have noticed that when groups start to grow larger than eight people, a team approach to leadership becomes vital and necessary to prevent leadership burnout.

Thus, groups larger than eight will need to consider putting two or more leaders in place to ensure no one experiences burnout. The same applies to groups led by a couple. If one couple takes on the weight of all the decision-making, too much planning/orchestrating of events, all the shepherding needs, etc., that couple will burn out. But if there are two or three couples involved in leadership (especially as groups grow to 30+ people), then the leadership team has enough creative and emotional capacity for it to be sustainable.

Foundation #4: A Living Network of Organisms

Since the 1800s, scientists have understood that tree stumps aren't actually dead. Many stumps can in fact remain alive for decades after the tree has been cut down, struck by lightning, or affected by disease. But it wasn't until recent years that scientists began to study why and how these stumps remain alive for so long. The sum of their findings was that a tree's root system sometimes fuses with the roots of other trees *if they are of the same species.* This collective of same species' fused roots creates what they refer to as a superorganism. If one tree is cut down or appears to be destroyed from the stump up, it may remain alive due to life flowing along the root system. Even more interestingly, during the day, substantial photosynthesis happens in the fully healthy trees, causing most of the nutrient-filled sap in the root system to flow toward the healthy upright trees; basically, it appears that nothing is happening in the dead-looking stump. But at night, when the photosynthesis process takes a break, the stump is infused with nutrient-dense sap, keeping it alive (even if no branches or leaves appear on the stump).

As scientists researched this further, they discovered this process isn't just to keep the stump alive (as the stump doesn't provide any photosynthesis for the superorganism), but that *the stump may actually function as a conduit between two healthy upright trees.* Imagine three trees: 1) healthy tall tree, 2) dead-looking stump (but still alive via the superorganism), and 3) unhealthy, suffering tall tree. In this scenario, the healthy tall tree photosynthesizes spectacularly during sunlight hours, but at night, reverses the nutrient-dense sap into the root system underneath the ground. The nutrients flow into the dead-looking stump and *through the stump roots* into the unhealthy, suffering tall tree that needs some help. The dead-looking stump can still provide life to other trees in the system! *Despite being struck down, it is not destroyed!* Despite its apparent lack, it is actually essential to the organic system underground. The dead-looking stump passes along life toward another tree that may be suffering and unhealthy, in need of the strengths of the superorganism.

Reflecting on this metaphor from nature has implications both for our communities and our structures. If we organize our systems to rely solely on professional clergy or one super-gifted individual, we miss out on the strengths and gifts that each person in the community has to offer. But if we are attentive to everyone—even those who may appear to be weak, cut off, or struck down, and we have eyes to see the grace of God coursing through their veins—then we tap into the power that God is bringing into his body because of the work of Jesus Christ and the Holy Spirit flowing through each one of us. How easy it is to write someone off due to some area of weakness that they seem to have; but by doing so, we fail to observe the grace that is actually present. However, if we have eyes to see what Jesus is doing, we will be attentive to how we construct our communities and our mission so that everyone can play a key role.

The kingdom of heaven is like a superorganism, empowering healthy trees, dead-looking (but more than alive) stumps, and weak trees to grow together. Ultimately, it is in the best interest of each tree to *fuse with others of similar species*. This illustrates what it means to be yoked with those with the same faith and Holy Spirit.

Foundation #5: The Peace Lily

Several years ago, Monica bought one of those "indestructible" plants, a Peace Lily, as she wanted to start having some indoor plants and decided it was best to start with an "easy" one. She researched how to care for it and did everything she thought it needed. She would water it once or twice a week, fertilize it regularly, and she even repotted it so it could grow bigger. Slowly, the plant started to wither. Monica tried everything she could to save it, but nothing worked. The problem was that she was caring for the plant *too much* and wasn't listening to what it needed. Eventually, it died.

Later, she was given a second chance with a new Peace Lily. This time, she knew how to observe what the plant needed and cared for it using the lessons learned with the first one. After two years of having the second plant, it started flowering. Monica was thrilled! In thinking back to the difference between her first plant that she had nurtured to death (literally), and the thriving one, it became obvious that the thriving plant required much less care and attention. You see, Peace Lilies are "easy" to care for because they don't need much. What may have felt like caring *less* for the plant was actually allowing it to grow best. Similarly, people and ministries do better when we care for them with open hands and trust in Christ and his work. Too often, we overreach for control or smother others with too much engagement.

It's easy to think we have figured out the vision for other people's lives. We can fall into a trap of wanting to micromanage their progress for them. But this is counterproductive because we are removing their ability to grow and strengthen on their own. By micromanaging others, we assume a much more powerful role than the Lord intends us to have! Let's remember his role in their lives and then see ourselves as conduits of grace rather than usurping him. Otherwise, we throw our identity into our work and misplace our own sense of worth in the achievement of another; and by doing so, we cause ourselves much more anger or grief over the "sins" of others or their stagnant progress. We must remember that God loves them more than we do. He has a much better and wiser plan for working out his grace in their lives. We can trust the Good Shepherd!

If we can truly trust the Lord with the well-being of those we are ministering to or those under our care, we also provide a tangible model of trust for them. When others see us fully trusting in God, our example speaks more than words can communicate. Let us be examples of faith, not those who meddle where it's not needed. This is how we can truly train others to trust God. And *this* is closer to true servant leadership. We are counterintuitively releasing and surrendering them to God's care, while being attentive to their needs. We learn to intercede in prayer for them, asking Christ to do his work. Often, our "problems" can be solved via prayer without needing to be humanly involved. In this way, we don't need to try to control every detail of their lives or get frustrated when the timing is slow; rather, we rely on him and walk in patience and joy, retaining incredible hope for those we care for.

Sure, it can be overwhelmingly painful and grievous to see people make the wrong decisions and go down paths of destruction, but if we can get appropriate perspective before intervening, then we will approach the situation with our eyes fixed on Christ, the author and finisher of our faith (Hebrews 12:2).[2] By fixing our gaze on Christ, we experience freedom and the ability to minister to others without focusing on our contributions and achievements. Instead of seeing people as potential "notches on our belt," we can see them as resting in the hands of the Father.

---

[2]   We recognize that sometimes intervention is absolutely necessary.

We also find ourselves loving people more freely and uncondi-tionally when we are not living for results. Friendships grow better when based on trust. Relationships become less transactional and more vital—more about the depth of love and delighting in the image of God in another person. As we do this, people remain people, not projects.

Loving people must always be sacrificial; when we don't surrender those we love to the Lord, we complicate the process and can even add unnecessary grief. Is there someone in your life that you need to lovingly release to God? Is there a ministry project you are unneces-sarily complicating with your own ambitions? Surrender this to the Father.

Just like the beauty of the living stump that fuses its roots to bring health to the underground superorganism, so too is the Peace Lily like the kingdom of heaven. You don't have to micromanage it; but those with patience and faith in the Lord will see the fruit of waiting on the Lord, and he will bring forth his kingdom.

ORGANIC SYSTEMS PARADIGMS

Paradigms are our guiding compass for contextual insight. Paradigms offer a solid framework, acting like a compass that orients us within our context, showing the possible directions we can travel. They shape how we see and interpret our surroundings, guiding the complex work of application.

Paradigm #1: Organic Concentration for Multiplication

Ken Boa emphasizes that concentration is crucial to multiplication.[3] Remember that Jesus focused on seventy-two, and especially on twelve, and out of those, especially on three. Robert Coleman makes a great point in *The Master Plan of Evangelism*, telling us, "Better to give a year or so to one or two people who learn what it means to conquer for Christ than to spend a lifetime with a congregation just to keep the

---

3   Boa, *Conformed to His Image*, 372.

program going."[4] This is one of those counterintuitive principles of Jesus' kingdom that requires intentional effort. If the Lord desires, we may have a greater impact on a global scale by focusing on just a few individuals than trying to reach the billions. One way to concentrate on a few people is to use the four spaces tool (intimate, small group, party, and public spaces) mentioned in the tools section below.

Paradigm #2: Building City Networks

In his book *Well Connected*, Phill Butler makes excellent points about the synergistic benefits of working with other Christian leaders in one's region.[5] It has often been said in church-planting circles that one of the most significant mistakes younger leaders make is to not get connected to older leaders in their city. We see this to be true. (And perhaps one of the most significant mistakes older leaders make is to remain disconnected from the movement.) If we are sensitive to the movement of God in our city, we will be looking for like-minded ministry partners that we can support, enable, and empower.

We personally participated in building a network or relational grid across Richmond, Virginia, and also in Denver, Colorado, and it's absolutely incredible to see the generosity that leaders show to one another. Until we began our work in Richmond, we had never seen it happen like that in any other city, but now we see it happening in many places globally. We believe it requires people to be willing to value the movement over their respective ministries. When they see the bigger picture, it causes them to work together—not just churches but denominations and ministry networks too. When leaders see things this way, it means they don't hold onto people, resources, or energy, or have a territorial mindset. It requires an abundance mentality as opposed to a scarcity mentality.

Personally, whenever we have arrived in a new city, we immediately take on a broad concern for the spiritual culture and movemental

---

4 Coleman, *The Master Plan of Evangelism*, 117.

5 Phill Butler, *Well Connected: Releasing Power, Restoring Hope Through Kingdom Partnerships* (Authentic Media, 2006).

activity. In Richmond, we began by meeting with everyone we could who might have insight into the city, its history, its religious history, and its current spiritual condition. We took note of those who were attentive to the Lord's work in the region and those who had eyes oriented to the kingdom. By focusing on and partnering with kingdom-minded people, we saw movements organically emerge. Sure, it had been happening long before we arrived, but now we were able to play a part in connecting the movement even more. And the strength of movements is in the friendships and relationships—they are the basis for movements and are organic in their own right.

To truly become a movement, power structures must be decentralized. When this happens, a movement takes on a new kind of power as it grows. A movement becomes a living, breathing, moving organism as the individual nodes form hubs and superhubs, and each operates with the vitality of the ethos/value system that sparked the movement in the beginning. We see this reality mirrored in the world of finance, as interestingly described by Sandra Navidi when she applies network science to global financial structures. In her book *SuperHubs*, she analyzes how global financial leaders connect, create a culture of friendship, act like a living movement together, and become almost impermeable to outsiders (for better or for worse).[6] Even though it is a secular book about finance and economics, its insights for a kingdom movement thinker are poignant. Imagine each person as a node in the network; then a small group or church could act like a hub; and perhaps larger ministry organizations or denominations act like larger hubs. The more large hubs that connect to a church, ministry, or person, the more that entity evolves into a superhub. The more connected a hub becomes, the more influence and power it wields, and the more other hubs want to connect to it.

Through our examination of a number of ministries and individuals globally, we have noticed a unique phenomenon concerning superhubs: They are willing to sacrifice greatly and give generously to those around

---

[6] Sandra Navidi, *SuperHubs: How the Financial Elite and Their Networks Rule Our World* (Nicholas Brealey Publishing, 2017).

them. That's a kingdom of heaven principle, isn't it? By giving away power, a different sort of power is acquired. For example, we know one individual who is connected to multiple denominations, multiple churches, multiple leaders and ministry networks, and has the ear of key leaders in each. This person takes the time to answer emails, return phone calls, step aside from other engagements in order to pour into leaders and support them, to bend over backward for the movement. As a result, this individual has huge influence that is invisible to most people.

People like this are connectors but also investors in others. They continue to have an eye on the big picture of what the Lord is doing. Because they can see this big picture, they maintain an optimism that most leaders don't have.

Try mapping your part of the movement. In our own practice, we frequently draw a movement map for our region, and it's beautiful to see what the Lord is doing. For our maps, we put our city at the center, and then list the peripheral cities on the corners of the page. We list which ministries, churches, denominations, leaders, servants, and key people are present in specific parts of the region. Then we draw lines showing how people connect. (This inevitably reveals how certain people still *need* to be connected to others, leading us to set up introductory meetings.) We write action steps for the various nodes and hubs and note interesting correlations in what we see the Lord doing in different places. Suddenly, it is like we are looking at a schematic of God's work in our region. In doing this practice, it always amazes us how much we can see the Lord doing in our city. Yet we also keep in mind there is much more we cannot even fathom! The Lord is always more at work than most of us can fully comprehend.

How could the Lord use you to further connect and build the movement in your city?

In many cities, missional practitioner networks are spontaneously emerging—often from a few missional practitioners regularly meeting to pray. Eventually, they invite more people, and friendships multiply. Some leaders even release valuable servants from their own ministries in order to help the movement. Some give to each other financially. Some give generously of their time to help in others' ministries. Synergy happens across the board. These groups may meet regularly; but more importantly, they are a highly relational network that doesn't disappear. Often these practitioners recommend that they meet someone else, introducing them, which typically results in new partnerships and kingdom endeavors. When one practitioner is hurting, others help out and shepherd each other. They share resources. Witnessing this developing organically has been one of the highlights of our ministry experience. There often is no official leader for these types of groups—they are organic. For example, on one missional practitioner network, we would take turns facilitating the gatherings. Recently, upon examining the web of connections from a "local hub," we realized that this hub (which has less than ten people actively involved) is actually significantly connected to over thirty churches/networks/denominations. It's mind-boggling to consider the impact of a tiny bit of organizing!

ORGANIC SYSTEMS TOOLS

Tools are the adaptable, practical methods that light our way. Like a handheld torch, tools illuminate specific areas of need or challenge, guiding our actions. Not every practice will be suitable for every situation. Therefore, careful discernment is crucial in selecting the right tool for the task. Once a particular tool effectively reveals solutions, we can apply it with increasing diligence and frequency, focusing our efforts where they are most needed.

Tool #1: The Four Spaces

The cultural anthropologist Edward T. Hall coined the term "proxemics," which explains the way we interact with one another depending on the size of a social group.[7] For our purposes, the size of a group may determine what the structure and intention will look like for the movement.

---

[7] Edward T. Hall, *The Hidden Dimension* (Bantam Doubleday, 1988).

- 1–3 people: Intimate space
- 4–12 people: Small-group space
- 12–50 people: Party space
- 50+ people: Public space

It seems that Jesus had the three (*intimate space*), the Twelve (which corresponds loosely to the *small-group space*), and then the broader Seventy-Two, (which would be a huge *party space* of people if they were all gathered). The masses (*public space*) were beyond that—the thousands.

Intimate space (1–3 people) is the place for transformation. It is a place for high accountability, high transparency, and life-on-life discipleship. This is where deeper spiritual friendships can occur. But if a group grows to over eight people, and you are still looking for that which can only come from an intimate space, you will find yourself lacking and inevitably complaining or criticizing the group for not providing for your needs.

Small-group space (4–12 people) is an excellent place for seekers to have the freedom to be affirmed for who they are, loved, and begin to experience real community. You might do this space around the table (as we see Jesus do in many places in the Gospels). The table can be a place for meals and deepening friendship but isn't necessarily an instructive environment. This could be an informal gathering of a few people who intend to go deeper relationally, though their individual desires for a deeper connection with Jesus may vary. Some may be exploring who Jesus is. We met a guy who planted churches around the world simply by starting up meals and centering them around exploring Jesus. He would leave the group when it had only a few people, making sure that at least two of them were committed to hosting meals and centering conversations on Jesus. Over the years, this man lost count of the hundreds of micro-churches he had planted just by having meals. Sounds too easy, doesn't it?

Party space (12–50 people) is excellent for less intense interactions and superficial engagement. This is a necessary part of life, as

Eugene Peterson explores in *The Contemplative Pastor*.[8] He speaks of a "ministry of small talk," acknowledging that most people live within the everyday details of their lives and need to connect at the level of small talk in order to build trust. Although many of us may dislike small talk, preferring to talk about the deeper things of life, we must recognize that people's lives are embedded and interwoven in those things that constitute what we may view as meaningless small talk. Therefore, it's important not to overlook the significance of meeting people where they are, patiently allowing them the time to gradually move toward deeper conversations.

Public space (50+ people) tends to be defined for us today as the large network of people we come into contact within our workplaces, neighborhoods, and communities. These might be people we meet only once, or who we're aware of in a broader context but don't regularly have the opportunity to speak to.

These spaces help us to understand how different sizes or groups work and how we can use this understanding to harness the power of socialization so that our times together have the right purposes. For example, some churches try to use the refreshments time after a Sunday service to build deep friendships in the congregation. These don't generally work as expected! Similarly, if we try to use a small-group space to deliver a sermon, it might not be the best use of the space. As a group, do you utilize all of these spaces? Are they functioning in a way that reflects their natural, social dynamics?

We can also think about these spaces as we seek to disciple new followers of Jesus. Most people will initially connect through a public or party space and will want to have built some connections and stronger relationships before they are comfortable in the small group setting. What spaces might you be able to create that are at the party size where you could connect with those beginning to explore faith in Jesus? It could be a social event, a connection through a sport or hobby activity, or involve meeting in a more public space like a park or café— anywhere that might engage people in the party space. Once you've

---

[8]   Peterson, *The Contemplative Pastor*, 111.

done this, think about what would be the natural invitation from this space to the small-group space (which might be a more overt discipleship group or faith exploration group)? And then how might you invite those wanting to grow in discipleship into the intimate space where they can journey more intentionally with two or three people?

We have seen many Christians adopt this idea and create rhythms around different social spaces in their movements—from children in Chile and Venezuela to a new believer in Europe to leaders in churches in the US. One young man we knew used his understanding of the social spaces to disciple many people, to the extent that we think his influence will be more than most church pastors could ever hope for. He simply worked disciple-making patterns into his natural rhythms of life, eating meals, hanging out with people, and pouring into deep relationships.

Tool #2: In, Out, Up

As mentioned in the discipleship chapter, we love this paradigm:

- **In:** The inward journey we take individually and communally into the love that the Father has for us; the awareness of who we are in him; and the building up of one another in love. This is the fellowship (sharing of faith) that we have with other believers. It is the spiritual union that we share with one another, experiencing the oneness that Jesus prayed for in John 17.
- **Out:** This is missional sent-ness—the apostolic journey into the world to proclaim the good news in word and deed. As a sent people, we can live this outward-ness both on our own and in community as we serve and love others in tangible ways.
- **Up:** Worship—the soul's true rest. The upward journey is the infinite pursuit of knowing God. We do this alone and in community.

Discipleship happens when all three of these rhythms are engaged. A community intentionally pursuing a balance in these three elements will be transformative, and it can be used to form a powerful rhythm for a group.

Tool #3: Multiplication

Beginning to meet with even two or three people, incorporating the tools within this book, means you are effectively planting a microchurch. If, after a few months, you have kept up these rhythms and your group is growing to five to eight people, you can begin identifying two or three people in the group who are emerging leaders and will begin multiplying the next group (not necessarily leaving the original group, unless they want to). We have seen that it is healthy for people to be able to begin new groups on the side rather than just *leaving* their current group, although both can work. By starting a new group on the side, you honor the current relationships; and you continue to shepherd those relationships well without just unplugging. As you multiply into several groups, you may want to think about structures for supporting the leaders of the groups, without placing too much burden upon them. These can be leadership huddles, or coaching groups where mentoring, prayer, and accountability is offered to those leading multiplied groups.

Each microchurch needs faithful contextualization, so how a group approaches these additional support structures will be particular to the needs of that group. We don't recommend a one-size-fits-all approach to this but rather, prayerful discernment of what is needed to supplement the emerging leaders and equip them to be faithful. For example, in one city, we started gathering all the leaders of groups monthly for about a year for mutual equipping, connecting, and support. We ate a meal together, shared victories and struggles, and prayed for one another. We also started gathering all the groups together quarterly for a big celebration where more cross-pollination could happen and folks could be exposed to the broader movement rather than just their specific microchurch.

As many leaders are now spread out across different countries, we have continued to do a monthly zoom call for the sake of encouragement and meeting deeply with God together.

Tool #4: APEST Environments

If it is going to be "this simple," how do you train people appropriately? How do you take care of the massive amount of counseling needs within the body *and* outside the body in the broader missional context? How do you make sure that multiplication actually happens appropriately? How do you mobilize to address systemic injustice in your city? How do you protect the integrity of the doctrine in these groups? How do you guard the missional DNA of these groups? How do you address the needs of the lost in your area?

APEST and its influence on creating environments is part of the answer. If each of the five voices can speak regularly into the body, with appropriate maturity and freedom, you will see the right environments created to answer those questions. Take a moment and reflect on how apostles can create a sending environment, prophets can create a challenging/stretching/growing environment, evangelists can create a welcoming environment, shepherds can create a nurturing environment, and teachers can create a learning environment.

If these voices speak into areas of need, they will help to ensure low-maintenance environments that meet needs. This isn't about high levels of seminary training or being biblical scholars. We have met pastors in Peru who were illiterate but had an incredible understanding of Scripture as it had been passed down to them orally—and they were very effective at making disciples. We have friends from China whose entire church had only a few pages of Scripture! Each month, their house church would take one page and trade it for another page of Scripture from another house church; yet their church thrived and multiplied. After years of China being closed to Christians, many thought that the remaining underground church would have weak doctrine; but as they began talking with various underground leaders, they found that they had actually formulated an exceptional quality of theological doctrine. How? The Holy Spirit![9] "Organic" can work.

---

[9] It is worth noting, the doctrine of the perspicuity of Scripture. This doctrine claims that Scripture has a certain degree of clarity regarding the main points, and that it is not too hard

Organic systems of ecclesia *have worked* globally throughout the entirety of church history. But in the West, we have somehow collectively forgotten certain parts of church history and certain aspects of the early church. Increasingly, at a global scale, followers of Christ are waking up to these things. We recently met some missionaries in Costa Rica who were talking about all six major themes of this book. When we asked them which authors they were reading to discover these things, they looked at us and said, "We began reading our Bibles with different eyes and suddenly everything made sense in ways we had never seen before!" They were discovering organic structures, missional/incarnational living, and movement thinking, all as a result of the Lord just bringing this to their awareness through his Word.

IT'S SCRIPTURAL. IT'S RATIONAL. IT'S TRANSFORMATIONAL.

Just look at the Gospels and Acts, and you will find extremely natural means of ministry and mission. It can feel shocking when you compare some modern church structures and complexities to the simplicity found in the natural ways revealed in Scripture. But please don't condemn those who are still caught up in the modern structures. They are contextualizing to certain crowds, and many of their hearts still desire to glorify God with excellence. In the kingdom of heaven, we need "all hands-on deck," so let's encourage those in other structures of church to focus on making disciples in natural ways that clearly link with the patterns found in Scripture.

All this is also quite rational. To get a simple message in front of billions of people, you can use mass media to spread that message broadly. But if we consider the phrase "make disciples," and examine the life of Jesus and the early church, we realize that "getting the message out" is only part of the goal. We are called to go beyond that. Making disciples requires passing on a particular set of spiritual genetic code and a way of life that is oriented around Jesus. From a

---

to understand the major points of Scripture, as the Lord has made these most essential truths available to those who would ask, seek, and knock!

purely sociological standpoint, developing communities that pass on this genetic code as naturally and spontaneously as possible is quite rational. Fortunately, the Holy Spirit is the ultimate Guardian of that genetic code. We just need to commit to reproducing that code all around us.

Transformationally, we have seen the "organic thing" be maximized way beyond mechanical or overly engineered things. We have seen more ministry around kitchen tables in messy kitchens than in some sanitized, perfect worship environments with massive budgets to create ideal "spiritual growth" opportunities. Pastors who have jumped into the organic way have felt freed up and seen more transformation in those around them (both outside and within the faith) than in decades of former traditional ministry. We have met many pastors, missionaries, and ministry leaders who have shifted toward naturally occurring means of servanthood and disciple-making. We always hear a few key themes in their assessments: 1) more freedom in their lives than ever before; 2) more love in their families than ever before; 3) more true disciples being made than ever before; and 4) most importantly, they discovered Jesus again and with more deeply renewed intimacy than ever before. When the Sunday service is reduced to a weekly corporate performance, it has a low transformational element to it, although the Spirit of God works in our weakness. However, a life of constant celebration of his presence is potent. Regular analysis of the forced engineering of people in social structures can be depleting, but parties and meals centered on Jesus *in our midst* have eternal impact.

6

DEEP COMMUNITY
Taking on Risks by Faith

 KEY IDEAS:

- We are made for deep(er) community, and community is both a cause and effect of movements.
- When we take on risk or an arduous journey together, we have the opportunity to grow in faith and experience new depths of true community.
- To grow deep community, we need smaller, intentional spaces.
- Growing healthy community requires patience and often involves pressing through relational difficulty. This process can yield incredible growth and provide an important opportunity to grow in maturity.
- Deep community requires and produces the fruit of the Spirit.

 SEE FOR YOURSELF

Read Acts and ask yourself: What does this book show us about the church as a community? Read through John and ask: What did Jesus model about community? Consider the risk that the early church took upon itself. How would this have caused them to bond deeply with one another?

To go further, read the book of Revelation. Ask yourself: What does the eternal community look like? Pay special attention to the corporate worship scenes in Revelation. You might also want to study all the Scriptures in the New Testament that refer to "one another," asking similar questions.

DEEP COMMUNITY FOUNDATIONS

Foundations are our unshakable core map, charting the terrain. Foundations provide the rock-solid theological principles that remain constant, regardless of the specific location or context we find ourselves in. They equip and prepare us for the journey, ensuring we have a reliable understanding of the fundamental landscape.

Foundation #1: Belonging

One of the most deeply felt human needs is belonging. When following Jesus together, a community can be the most transformative aspect of someone's walk in Christ; but many who have walked away from church have done so because their Christian community hurt them. Deep community is both a fruit of all of the preceding topics in this book and a necessary ingredient for reinforcing them. Deep community is required for movement to happen. Here is the logical continuum: If we are Jesus-centered and Jesus-permeated (yielding as Jesus takes up residence in our hearts), then we are followers of Jesus; and he commanded his followers to go and make disciples. According to Jesus himself, if we follow him, we will fish for people—incarnational living with a missional strategic mindset. As we do these things, the movement will expand (movement wisdom), and we will see natural relationships developing (organic systems), which simultaneously requires *and* creates opportunity for deep community. Deep community that is Jesus-centered will produce disciples who produce disciples. Deep community that is Jesus-permeated will have missional and incarnational impulse as the Spirit of God moves within the fullness of the body to be the body. Deep community is a *must* when expansive movements occur because movements thrive on the fringe or the "edge of chaos" itself.

Foundation #2: Friendship Sparks Movements

C. S. Lewis shared deep insights about community and movements. In his book *The Four Loves*, he mentions that no movement has ever started without a few deep friendships.[1] The kernel of a movement (good or evil) is a few people agreeing on a particular set of truth claims about the world around them. They become deeper friends when their assessment of this set of truth claims puts them at odds with the surrounding culture/environment. Lewis said that a friendship is born when one looks at another and says, "What? You too? I thought I was the only one!"

"Love" can be considered in a few categories, including an initial general sense of well-being and care for those around us (Lewis calls this "affection"), which increases toward companionship when people partner together for a particular cause. Friendship arises when we notice that someone else sees the world in a similar way to us. Lewis mentions that when the Greeks set the foundation for modern mathematics, it was based on a few friends who kept coming together to discuss the ideas that no one else seemed to care about. (The original geeks were Greeks!) He notes that Marxism spread this way too—a few people who viewed economics, class, and culture differently from the rest, who met together and endlessly obsessed about these views. Deep in the core of a movement, good or bad, are a few people who can't shake their particular perspective of reality, which unifies them as friends.

Lewis points out that while *eros* (romantic love) has two people focusing on each other, friendship is a love that causes people to look outward together, side by side. They want others to join them in their

---

[1] C. S. Lewis, *The Four Loves* (HarperOne, 2017), 100.

cause. This is a deep desire built into human nature: It is not good that man is alone (Genesis 2:18); two are better than one and three are better than two; a threefold cord is not easily broken (Ecclesiastes 4:12). Movements begin when we tap into this principle. When two or three come together in the name of Christ, there he is also (Matthew 18:20).

In our own practice, one of the things we regularly talk about as we make disciples is simply helping people learn to be friends with others. In a fragmented, hyper-individualistic, neurotic world, this is quite countercultural. Imagine the power of a few friends getting together for the purposes of Jesus and then spreading this goodness out toward others. This is how movements happen. It is organic and natural, and it doesn't take much funding to cause friendships to happen.

Foundation #3: Risk and Bonding

What epic story doesn't end with the survivors or victors knowing each other better than before? When people take on risk together, when their survival depends upon working together, when the task seems impossible, people come out the other side transformed. Think of how people come back from a camping trip looking at each other differently. Think of how lifelong friendships can sometimes be formed when random strangers endure a crisis or a dangerous scenario together. Think of *The Lord of the Rings* and how the fellowship grew together through their arduous journey. The same goes for most stories that have captivated our world: When people go through crazy things together and endure, they come out changed. They are not just changed by the experience but by each other. When a community of Jesus-followers follow Jesus into his mission in their context, they will find that the journey can be arduous, difficult, and seemingly impossible. Following Jesus together, on his mission, often puts us up against seemingly impossible odds and immense spiritual warfare. If we emerge faithful together, we will be stronger than ever and understand more of why Jesus refers to the body as "the body."

Foundation #4: Giant Sequoias

If you stand before one of the giant Sequoias, you will never forget their majesty. These trees are large enough that people have carved roads *through* the tree base! Some of them are taller than the Statue of Liberty. Being so tall, Sequoias bear the load of intensely forceful winds. Yet these trees rarely fall over, and live for centuries, withstanding all sorts of weather conditions and even forest fires.

The secret to the Sequoias' success is their root system. Their roots intertwine to create an underground webbed foundation. When intense winds are pressing hard against the tree, the tree shifts and begins to *pull on the root system underground for support.* Think of it like fingers interwoven to maximize potential strength. On its own, a single Sequoia has significantly lower odds of survival. Sequoias that grow too far away from the cluster are almost bound to fall over in a storm or die (unless other Sequoias begin to grow close enough to start supporting it), because an individual Sequoia's roots don't go down deep enough to fully support the tree. The roots are shallow and wide! But Sequoias weren't created to stand alone. Their majesty is enabled and empowered to the maximum when they stand together in tree communities, their root systems strengthening one another. When strong winds come, the Sequoias sway but pull from an intricate web of interlocking roots that provides an exponentially strong foundation. The beauty is that no one would know this by looking at the tree itself. You need to look underground, or rely on those who have completed extensive research, to understand the root system.

This is what it is like within the kingdom of heaven. Our systems and our communities must be interdependent. There is a reason we are called the body and the household. We admit, once you rely on people and they let you down, you may never want to rely on people again; but when you rely on the Lord to work through the children of God, you view people in their proper place, and you discover the strength of deep community—community that has spiritual ties beyond what is visible.

Foundation #5: Deep Community—*Not* What You May Think

Deep community and oneness are high ideals. Who can attain it? None of us, without the grace and indwelling of the Holy Spirit! This is why we focus on "in" and not just "out, up, and beyond" in our rhythms. This need for deep community is why we must have both party spaces and small-group spaces. This is why we must go deeper from small-group spaces to intimate spaces to develop transformational relationships.

One of the most transformative communal ministry experiences we had was in Costa Rica, where our ministry failed according to the measurements we were tracking. Our church plant failed. Most of those who had committed to the team never showed up. People rejected us constantly. But the Lord brought us together as a team in miraculous ways. We cried together; we began sharing much more deeply with one another; we loved one another and sacrificed in great ways; we experienced a deep unity and deep awareness—knowing—of one another. The pain created a common experience that took us beyond our relationships in other circles. The corporate failure and rejection tested our commitment to one another and our commitment to our own self-interests. It had a purging effect on our selfishness, which was replaced with pure love for Jesus and one another. We experienced worship at levels that many of us had never experienced prior to that time. Our group consisted of three ethnicities—African American, white American, and Costa Rican (Central American)—but by the end of our time together, we felt a oneness. Deep community is a fruit for those who dare to persevere. Deep community requires violation of our own egocentrism and self-focus. Deep community both requires and creates self-forgetfulness.

When a group of people faces danger and risk together, it creates a dynamic social change within the group. If they choose to commit to each other, they can bond in the face of adversity and emerge as different people with a different communal identity. This is a well-documented social phenomenon that has powerful implications for the church when it is unified around a common mission.[2]

---

[2] For those who are interested in understanding these dynamics a bit more, I recommend Alan

In the same way, when we depend on relationships for the survival of the team, we can feel that it will require all of us to make it work. This has an interesting effect on "attendance." People become so committed to one another that they begin to have regular cadences of life with each other, in such a way that "attendance" isn't an issue because their lives are covenanted to one another. Family becomes a more important reality than any blood relationships because we see family as those who do the will of Christ. One friend, who had lost all of his immediate family, would often come to groups saying that these people were his family, and he followed through with the relational commitments that this sort of language would entail. But most people haven't experienced this place of belonging *yet*. Let us change that fact as we go forth together!

Foundation #6: The Mechanics and Spirituality of Trust[3]

A brief word on trust. Trust is always a risk—but even more so for those who step into the frontlines of mission. Deep community also means that there can be deep wounds. Many Christian leaders get burned and shut down or cease loving and trusting those around them. It is vital for the Christian leader to examine how "trust" is impacting their life and relationships.

In talking with a friend engaged in missions in numerous countries in Africa, we identified two aspects of trust:

- The *mechanics* of trust: How we trust others appropriately without creating significant problems.
- The *spirituality* of trust: How we engage our hearts before

---

Hirsch's chapter "*Communitas*, Not Community" in *The Forgotten Ways*. For any leader with strategic multiplication in mind, this chapter has huge potential for unearthing wise strategies that honor the Lord. See also, Michael Frost and Alan Hirsch, *The Faith of Leap: Embracing a Theology of Risk, Adventure and Courage*, revised ed. (100 Movements Publishing, 2025).

3   After a dialogue with a missionary in Africa about trust, Jeremy wrote the following blog for The V3 Movement: http://thev3movement.org/2019/04/16/the-mechanics-and-spirituality-of-trust/ (accessed April 25, 2025).

Christ so that we respond in the present without being triggered by hurts from the past.

Trust is a big issue in Africa, especially when you are in remote places and need to rely on others for vital elements of your vision/project. If you cannot trust someone, you may be unable to complete a project. After a few bad experiences with "trusting people," it is easy to stop thinking anyone is trustworthy. But imagine how that would destroy your ministry! How will you ever get anything done if you can't trust anyone? Do it all yourself? Really? How is that biblical? How does that fit in with this idea of being members of one body, filled with faith, hope, and love? So, we see that trust is vital. How then do we discern if someone is trustworthy?

Three elements are needed for trust:

- **The trust of *integrity*:** Does this person have the right intention and motivation?
- **The trust of *competency*:** Can they do the task? Are they available? Are they operational?
- **The trust of *chemistry*:** Do we have enough chemistry to collaborate?

Someone might have two of these elements, but if the third is missing, there could be difficulties.

We once heard an intercultural studies professor say we have two tools when learning to trust: testing and time. We regularly need to test out the trustworthiness of those with whom we are working, and that takes *lots* of time. The tests often need to come in small doses over a prolonged period in order to see how competent someone is (faithful/available/teachable/operational). Of course, time also fleshes out the defects that may be hidden away in someone's character.

Many of us know all too well the experience of entrusting something important to someone who can "talk the talk," only to find out later that this had disastrous consequences. Various people making disciples have told us it takes them more than a year, and sometimes two years, before they feel they have a foundation of trust in a potential leader. With a timeline that long, it seems like multiplying could take forever! This is where the spirituality of trust becomes even more essential for deep community building.

Having been burned a few times (and sometimes burnt by those in deep community with us), we are more skeptical than we used to be. But the Lord is teaching us that having deep community requires we trust people appropriately and put ourselves at potential risk within the confines of faith-filled discernment. The Lord is teaching us the importance of forgiving past hurts to have solid, appropriate trust in current situations. If you feel similarly, allow yourself time to discern why you may be struggling with trust, and seek the Lord (Psalm 139) to see how he may be leading you to a place of deeper healing and faith in him.

Ultimately, if we are going to trust people so that we can achieve the work/vision that God has called us to, we will need to:

- Be cautious and build wisdom and discernment.
- Walk by faith.
- Elevate the role of patience and hope-filled prayer in our lives.
- Be willing to take calculated risks out of love for God and others.
- Learn how to lovingly understand others and communicate effectively.

These eternal values provide the true basis for healthy working relation-ships and kingdom partnerships.[4]

Foundation #7: Fruit of the Spirit

Deep community will have:

Love—wanting the best for another person. Love is the uncon-ditional intention, affection, and "bendedness" toward another, to

---

[4] We recommend reading Duane Elmer, *Cross-Cultural Connections: Stepping Out and Fitting in Around the World* (InterVarsity Press, 2002).

will and to do that which is truly best for another's entire well-being. This involves feelings, yet it is able to operate objectively beyond mere feelings. It involves the element of respect for the personhood and will of the other, not forcing ourselves upon them. Love is a wise and humble respecter of the appropriate boundaries of personhood.

Joy—the deep resolve of hope and the conviction that goodness is always ahead, no matter what, that nothing is beyond redemption, and that love (God is love) will ultimately win out.

Peace—the inner strength of wholeness, a certainty beyond human understanding alone, a solidity and reality that extends into the whole being and brings all the parts into one; lacking confusion, full of assurance, grounded in a dependence that God is in control and knows best and loves best and that his paths are trustworthy. Choosing to lean not on our own understanding, but in all our ways—in every detail of our lives—seeing him and his involvement, and paying attention to his involvement, knowing he will set our paths in the appropriate and best direction.

Patience—the perspective that enables great endurance, that truly knows the nature of *all* reality. The knowledge that God will prevail; his loving kindness will endure forever; Jesus and his ways can be trusted; the Comforter will shepherd us through all things toward eternally green pastures and still waters (here on this earth and into eternity); and his goodness and mercy will follow us, surround us, and guide us toward endless depths.

Kindness—the purity of heart that overflows toward others, loving the image of God in them, seeing God's print on his work of art, caring to cultivate that artwork for the eternal beauty that he has put his signature on. Kindness has no thought for self, only for the tender mercy of God flowing toward others.

Goodness—those things which are of the most excellent nature, the things seated above, where Christ is (Colossians 3:1). Whatever is praiseworthy, whatever is noble, whatever is right, whatever has depth of eternal truth to it—this is goodness.

Faithfulness—the fullness of confidence and trust in the ways of Jesus, yielding all the fruits of goodness as we persevere in these ways.

Faithfulness is a loyal commitment to continually abide and remain in his heart, with his eternal values and perspective.

Gentleness—the wisdom for applying all the fruit of the Spirit. Gentleness is the care, the cautious caress, that knows how love needs to be uniquely applied to a situation.

Self-Control—the power and strength of perseverance in the fruits. It is not merely the ability to control ourselves but rather the ability to let the Holy Spirit control us, to walk in the Spirit with temperance, with the wisdom of knowing when to move/act and when to refrain, how much he is asking for, and how he wants it done.

Scripture tells us that no law can rail against these things (Galatians 5:23). These fruits are evidence of the presence of the Holy Spirit. Where they truly exist, the Spirit of God is at work. Let us press into these fruits, meditate upon their beauty, and let these ultimate master-pieces shape our hearts more into his image. When this happens, our communities will be known by their love; and we will always abound in the work of the Lord, overflowing with goodness and the fruit of righteousness toward one another. *Love brings joy and peace. When you have love, joy, peace, and patience, you will see all the other fruits evident as well. Where one of these fruits is truly overflowing, the others will also be present and overflowing.*

Gratitude has a place here as well. The power of gratitude is infinite. When we are grateful, we stop looking at ourselves and our problems. Gratitude leads us out of self-pity toward a right under-standing of and perspective on the circumstances around us. Gratitude is worship. Thankfulness requires humility because while pride says, "I deserve," humility says, "Thank you. You gave." Books could be written on the endless power and applications of gratitude.[5] Our lives will be transformed if we grasp its power.

Our communities will also be transformed if we grasp the power of gratitude. In gratitude, there is no condemnation toward others.

---

[5] See Ann Voskamp, *One Thousand Gifts: A Dare to Live Fully Right Where You Are* (Thomas Nelson, 2011).

True gratitude is a powerful, strong, resilient perspective that shakes the foundations of this world.

To neglect the Spirit and his fruit is to violate movement and to undermine true discipleship. If we do this, we lose community and move away from kingdom movement. Walk in the Spirit, and these fruits will grow with increasing power in your life—their beauty will shine like the stars!

DEEP COMMUNITY PARADIGMS

Paradigms are our guiding compass for contextual insight. Paradigms offer a solid framework, acting like a compass that orients us within our context, showing the possible directions we can travel. They shape how we see and interpret our surroundings, guiding the complex work of application.

Paradigm #1: Forming, Storming, Norming, Performing

In 1965, psychologist Bruce Tuckman described various stages of inevitable movement within a team that can produce great risk but also great health for those who persevere.[6] These are forming, storming, norming, and performing. In *The Church as Movement*, Woodward and White provide excellent insight for how Tuckman's stages can impact missional communities. They note that every community will go through times of forming (recruiting, coming together, vision building, ethos, and DNA-setting), but after a period of time, storming inevitably occurs.[7]

If you are not ready for the storming phase in your community, you will most likely run away because it really sucks! Storming is often ugly and painful. While the process of storming might be triggered by external pressures, the storming dynamic is centered around the internal workings and relationships of the group. Storming can happen

---

[6]   Bruce Tuckman, "Developmental Sequence in Small Groups," *Psychological Bulletin* 63(6), 1965, 384–99.

[7]   Woodward and White, *The Church as Movement*, 100–104.

when someone doesn't like the culture of the group or feels they don't fit in, leading them to either act out (fight) or become regularly absent (flight). Sometimes storming happens to one individual while the rest of the group is norming together (moving toward similar patterns, values, and rhythms). Other times, a few individuals within the group become divisive. Storming can happen due to theological disagreements, methodological disagreements, cultural differences, personality differences, selfishness, or more devious motivations. Sometimes storming occurs in a way that requires intense confrontation.[8] This can scare many people and deters them from pushing through with the aim of forming deeper community.

Because intense confrontation is the price to pay for deep community, most people tend to run away from it. Many other choices just feel better, *faster*, and deliver quicker results (hence the world of addictions that results from isolation). Our goal is to draw people toward *life*. Jesus first loved us, so we can love others. Jesus forgave us, so we can forgive others. It might seem simplistic to say that, but it's eternally powerful! If people are to experience *real* maturity and the beautiful, eternal delights that come from community and growth, they need to be drawn in and unconditionally loved. They need to get through the barrier of their hindrances to deep community. This is easier for some than others. The good news is that Jesus has created the opportunity for us to be reconciled (brought back into restored relationship) with God. As we receive this gift, we can extend the same reconciliation to others. We are ambassadors for Christ, imploring the world to be reconciled to God. Even more strongly, God is imploring the world, pleading with the world, through us, to be brought back into his divine community (2 Corinthians 5).

When people know in advance that storming is a reality (an inevitable one in a community), they can lay seeds of hope to get through the storming phase. Caught off guard, most people can't understand

---

[8] See Stone et al., *Difficult Conversations: How to Discuss What Matters Most*, 10th anniversary ed. (Penguin, 1990). See also, Susan Scott, *Fierce Conversations: Achieving Success in Work and in Life, One Conversation at a Time* (Piatkus, 2017).

what's happening; but once they are well-prepared, people are ready to engage, even if they don't yet have all the tools to push through. Hope reminds them in advance: Hard relational time is coming, and we can make it through together in order to have better relationships.

A key to survive the storming stage: Get the junk out of your own eye before you call it out in someone else's! When you are offended, ask yourself why and what may need to change *in you* (even when the other person has done you an injustice). "What would need to change in me and in my heart for me to be able to love this person rather than be so offended?" Ask the Lord, "How do you want me to love this person through this offense?" When storming happens, we must humble ourselves, not criticize others, pray, and then pray some more; ask the Lord how he wants us to depend on his Spirit and grow through the process. Ask him what would be *best* for the health/joy/peace of the other person/rest of the group. If we commit to these actions first, we are ready to listen rather than defend, and to aim for outcomes that build up everyone involved.

For those who make it through a storming phase, there will be movement toward *norming* and ultimately *performing* together (yielding great fruit of relational union and building relational equity). True strength is a product of deep community. Again, most people will never experience true strength until they overcome their independence and learn interdependence and the kind of teamwork that excels beyond any individual—to become the beauty of the collective body.[9]

Paradigm #2: Adjourning, Transforming

A further addition to Tuckman's stages includes the opportunity for groups to consider adjourning or transforming. In the communities we have been part of, we describe these as healthy "beyond" conversations.

---

[9] *The Peacemaker* by Ken Sande has an excellent appendix for resolving conflict. Ken Sande, *The Peacemaker: A Biblical Guide to Resolving Personal Conflict* (Baker, 2004). The book is worth having just for that appendix! We also recommend lengthy time prayerfully studying Acts 15. One additional resource: Peacemaker Ministries has some excellent resources for being peacemakers in a biblical way. See www.peacemaker.net for some excellent, simple steps.

Every group needs a healthy opportunity to end. Every group needs the chance to pause for a period of time or to transform into something new. Rather than dragging a group on beyond its natural lifespan, it is good to adjourn and begin refocusing on new areas.

Paradigm #3: Organic and Spontaneous

Building deep community doesn't only look like meeting around a schedule but also gathering in spontaneous and unplanned ways. We can commit to grow in deep community with specific times, but there must also be an understanding that life-on-life interaction will increase and decrease in frequency as needed. There are times and rhythms in each person's life and capacity that will require them to sometimes be in deeper community on a daily basis, and sometimes be apart from others for periods of time.

Ecclesiastes is an excellent book for unpacking the reality of community. It contains great wisdom about vanity, the appointed and allotted time(s) for everything, the enjoyment of life, and truly respecting the Lord. Each of these has great bearing on our engagement in community.

There are appointed times for a significant increase in life-on-life involvement (they broke bread together daily in Acts 4), and yet there are times when solitude is vital for the health and balance of the soul as it grows Christ-ward.

Everything is *beautiful* in its appointed time. We don't need to *force* our communities to meet weekly. We can live in rhythms that allow for freedom and for life to be life. If we force our schedules to dominate our relational rhythms, we can lose sight of the beauty of relationships and of just *being* together, replacing this with transactional, achievement-focused community (where the purpose is to always see something happen, make plans for the next activity, or achieve some goal together). Churches can suffer from a toxic transactional lens for finding purpose within their communities. Freedom tells us that it can be different. Ecclesiastes reminds us that we cannot enjoy *anything* unless it is given to us to enjoy from the good hand of a good God (Ecclesiastes 5:19). This applies especially to community.

☼ DEEP COMMUNITY TOOLS

Tools are the adaptable, practical methods that light our way. Like a handheld torch, tools illuminate specific areas of need or challenge, guiding our actions. Not every practice will be suitable for every situation. Therefore, careful discernment is crucial in selecting the right tool for the task. Once a particular tool effectively reveals solutions, we can apply it with increasing diligence and frequency, focusing our efforts where they are most needed.

Tool #1: Difficult Conversations

In his book *Difficult Conversations*, lawyer Douglas Stone describes how to break through relational difficulties toward peace and reconciliation.[10] The following is inspired loosely by his book and adapted based on some of our own additional study and experience.

The best way to navigate relational tensions is to take a learning stance. We must learn more about the other person, ourselves, what is happening, and how we can move forward. A culture of learning creates a culture of opportunity—opportunity for maturity, strength, growth, and to know Christ who is the ultimate reconciler. If we approach things in this manner, then when a storm arises within a relationship, our minds will become trained to see the storm in almost the same way as we might see the spiritual disciplines—as an opportunity for us to die to our flesh and be transformed from the former glory into a deeper glory. Likewise, this is the same opportunity available to the other person, but they may need our loving help to see it as such. They need to know that they are loved.

Three basic conversations need to take place when relational difficulty (storming) arises: 1) the "what happened" conversation, 2) the feelings conversation, and 3) the identity conversation. Once these three have been worked through and identified, the "solution-oriented direction" (a phrase Jeremy's dad is known for in his counseling) can

---

[10] Stone et al., *Difficult Conversations*.

be identified, structured (mapping out a planned, prepared response), and entered into.

The "what happened" conversation. When discussing what happened, both parties must be willing to understand the other side first before aiming to be understood. This isn't about who is right or wrong. This is about how people perceive what happened. (Sometimes their perceptions may be skewed!) The more mature person will not need to defend themselves in many cases, but rather choose to press into the areas where perceptions are wrong and identify what underlying level of "hurt" or brokenness is at work in the other person. The more mature person will undergo identification with Christ: being accused, perhaps wrongly, but not defending themselves. We must also be willing to admit where we have contributed to the problem. This allows each party to see a conceptual map of contributing factors, which is essential to helping both people (in many cases) see that there is much more going on than just two people disagreeing. Perhaps both are hurting due to various other factors and are therefore unified along other lines that they had previously overlooked due to their own pain.

Even with these truths in mind, there is something to be said about boundaries in these situations. A mature person can see through emotive terms or verbal attacks and not take offense; but if the conversation becomes abusive, boundaries must be set.[11] Even so, we mustn't forget that the cross of Christ was the ultimate violation of boundaries,

---

[11] An intriguing example is Acts 16:22–40, where the Apostle Paul is beaten and imprisoned, but afterward he mentioned that he was a Roman citizen, which alarmed the officials. One must wonder if Paul could have avoided this beating/imprisonment if he had mentioned his citizenship earlier and thereby established a boundary to protect himself? Either way, we see Paul establish this boundary later in Acts 22:25–29, when he informs his accusers of his citizenship, and they decide not to beat him. (Perhaps he had learned a lesson from the first beating?) These two examples serve as an instructive example: Perhaps there are times when we need to set boundaries to protect ourselves. Perhaps there are also times when we should not set boundaries. Here is where discernment and wisdom are vital to our growth, self-protection, and self-sacrifice. Cloud and Townsend's book on boundaries is a great place to start when discerning how to set boundaries in our own lives. Dr. Henry Cloud and Dr. John Townsend, *Boundaries: When to Say Yes, How to Say No to Take Control of Your Life,* updated and revised ed. (Zondervan, 2017).

so there is a tension with this principle. If anyone wants to gain their life (perhaps by self-protective boundaries), they will lose it; but if anyone is willing to lose their life for his sake, they actually gain it (Matthew 16:25). Don't excuse selfishness under the name of "boundaries."

The feelings conversation. Moving beyond asking "What happened?" this conversation turns to the issue of how people are feeling. This is where we learn to have compassion for the other person. We need to invite them to share their feelings with us if there is any hope for mutual understanding or reconciliation. After you have allowed the other person to share their feelings, discern if they will allow you to share yours, or to share your understanding of the situation. There may be more that they feel they need to say before you can do this. Surrender your pride and allow them to say what they need. The aim is for you to move toward understanding their heart. But make sure to create space and ask them to hear you out afterward so that they can understand your perspective. You do them an injustice by not sharing your perspective with them (if they are open to hearing it).

The identity conversation. Finally, it is vital to have the identity conversation to see what is at stake. Depending on the situation, there might be a *lot* at stake. Talking about this helps to identify common values that can unite both people. This brings both parties to a place of agreement (or awareness of areas needing further clarity and unity) about the value of the relationship, wider community, pursuing maturity, witnessing to others, and Jesus being honored. While the DNA of the gospel must permeate each step, this phase especially needs to be gospel infused. We work toward peace because Jesus demonstrated to us how far he was willing to go to create peace; we can have these conversations in his strength because he first loved us.

From this point forward, if both people have been willing to put in the work and respect one another, then they are ready to identify common ground and the foundation(s) for moving forward toward solutions. It will be those who live by the Spirit who look to restore and initiate solutions.[12]

---

[12] Galatians 6:1.

A word on pettiness: If you are the one being offended, or if you see something as "sin" and think that it needs to be called out, take time to pray and listen to the Holy Spirit. Consider the fruits of the Spirit and how you might allow them to reign in your life, and how to treat someone with love, peace, and goodness. Also, take time to ask yourself, as Ken Sande puts it, "How much [will it] cost (emotionally, spiritually, and financially) to continue a conflict instead of simply settling it?"[13] The ancient wisdom in Proverbs tells us that it is to your glory to overlook a slight from someone else—it is glorious to be willing to overlook the small things (Proverbs 19:11). You need to discern if an issue is something worth bringing up, or if it is something you can pray through and settle individually before the Lord. If you feel any condemnation toward the other person, your own heart issue is more dangerous than *all* their sin.

Tool #2: Closed, Covenanted Groups

There are many types of groups with different intentions that can serve the purpose of making disciples. Jesus himself recruited the Twelve and then used opportunities designed for ministering to, pouring into, and equipping just those twelve disciples. He didn't neglect others but paid special attention to that specific (closed) group. Bill Hull and many others in missional circles emphasize the vital importance of closed, covenanted groups.[14] If a group has a common mission, they will excel by utilizing the tool of covenant and creating a closed community.

Not every community has to be like this, but it is a vital option for a team aiming to serve a specific group of people. Hull identifies a few benefits of closed groups: "An open group can't provide the

---

13 Sande, *The Peacemaker*, 264.

14 A covenanted group is one that has some degree of mutual agreement (verbal or written) to which everyone is expressing a loving commitment to faithfulness toward each other, and some degree of communal, predictable, and loyal participation.

necessary structure and accountability" and "closed groups provide an atmosphere for practicing spiritual disciplines."[15]

Internal mission drift and culture deterioration happen more easily when a group integrates newcomers. This is where it can be helpful for us to identify the different spaces we operate within. (See the previous chapter.) It is often best to allow newcomers to fit into a broader circle (public space and party space). This allows for much more open fluidity and for strangers to become friends. The discipleship of a core team can take place in a smaller space (small-group space and intimate space). Keeping this space closed for a period of time (not indefinitely, as that creates an entirely new set of problems) allows you to create a culture of intentional equipping without needing to explain everything to each new person who joins. The smaller spaces also allow for deeper relational continuity that an open group may not be able to maintain.

Consider this dynamic: If you start a community with three to eight people, with the goal of reaching a broader group, you will want to recruit, set the DNA/tone/posture, and regularly meet for peer coaching, equipping, and practicing spiritual disciplines together. However, every time a new person joins, the internal culture shifts. If forming, storming, norming, and performing phases are happening in the life cycle of the group, each new person who joins creates additional storming realities because they are coming into a group that has already formulated an internal culture and value system. Keeping this smaller group closed allows space for the life cycle of the group to progress.

Tool #3: Community in Six Streams

In chapter two we mentioned six streams of Christianity (c.f. Foster, *Streams of Living Water*). They are as follows:

---

[15] Hull, *The Complete Book of Discipleship*, 233–234.

- Biblical/Evangelical
- Holy Spirit/Charismatic
- Holiness/Virtue
- Prayer/Contemplative
- Incarnational/Sacramental
- Compassion/Justice

For communities to function well, we need to understand how these streams impact so much of our church life. For those who don't have a church background, many of these streams and their accompanying practices are unfamiliar and might even seem quite strange. Imagine someone with no experience of the charismatic coming into a charismatic church. Many times, they are scared away because of language, cultural objects, rhythms, and practices that differ from their denominational background. Rather than letting these differences scare people away from deeper community, our awareness of one another's background and experiences will enable us to love each other and bring the strengths of our differences to bear on one another's lives. Awareness of these streams also enables us to avoid imbalance with any one stream in particular. Imbalance will hinder movement. But if a community or movement is balanced, then it will showcase the strengths of each—we will need to forge kingdom partnerships with Jesus-followers across the streams.

It is also vital for each community to know how they are going to move forward in their discipleship practices. How will they do the inward journey together? The outward mission? The upward worship? Here is a simplification of what the outward and upward can look like in each of the six streams:

- **Biblical/Evangelical:** Those with this background are prone to enjoy upward worship in the form of Bible studies and sharing what the Lord is teaching them. Their outward expression may often be communicating the gospel via words to those around them.
- **Holy Spirit/Charismatic:** These individuals will find worshipful expression in singing, praise, and dancing. Their outward

expressions of ministry will often be inclined toward sensing the Spirit's lead toward individuals, praying for people on the spot, sometimes even doing different forms of street evangelism.

- **Holiness/Virtue:** Some from this background will focus on how our lives as a whole are an act of holy worship unto the Lord— how we live our lives *is* our worship. Their outward ministry will be about being an example and a presence of God's goodness to those around them.
- **Prayer/Contemplative:** Those from this background may find places of prayer to be the best form of worship, in silence and solitude but also in community prayer groups. Reaching outward may also be seen as starting from a place of prayer, intercessory groups, gatherings simply to pray for the city or to pray with people who are far from God.
- **Incarnational/Sacramental:** These people will focus on the beauty of God in all places and in all actions, seeing that virtually anything can be made holy if we do it as unto the Lord (1 Corinthians 10:31). They may also view outward ministry as a ministry of presence, being among people as a positive force and investing the gospel in the lives of those around them, particularly through actions.
- **Compassion/Justice:** These individuals may find worship to be connected with the gospel's proclamation of freedom and celebrating the wholeness God brings with this freedom. These people will demonstrate outward ministry through changing systems, freeing the impoverished and broken, and going to those who are most hurt and oppressed.

Tool #4: Outreach

A deep community influences and impacts others through incarnational love. By living out the good news, they see kingdom transformation in those who come into contact with their group. We have seen this in many ways over the years and around the world. The shyest and most socially awkward people can become warriors of the faith as a result of deep communities that loved, cared for, affirmed, and called them upward and outward. Antisocial people, characterized by hatred, bitterness, and anger can become loving, caring, gentle, and humble servant leaders because of the perseverance of a loving and deep community. We have also seen friends who were outside the faith slowly become enculturated by Jesus through the constant servan-thood and active love of multiple members of the body of Christ.

Imagine what it does to someone alone and isolated when suddenly their "friend group" is filled with people who are effusive in love and the fruit of the Spirit, the bond of peace, and a commitment to care for one another, no matter what. The weakest will become profound and potent; the most hurt can become the caretakers of souls; the most dejected and self-loathing can become a soul winner who shines brightly like the stars!

Tool #5: Means of Deepening

If we are truly faithful to God's work and operate with his DNA, fruitfulness will result. We have mentioned various tools as means of honoring Jesus' DNA. None of those should be seen as magic formulas; rather, they are tools for the purpose of investing faithfully into his kingdom and being wise stewards of our time, energy, and resources. If we want to deepen community, a few additional tools for creating incredible depth include retreats, missions trips, adventures, faith-stretching/sacrificial goals for a community to work toward, and commitments with one another.

Retreats: Over the years, we have researched and experimented with dozens of styles of retreats and have found that most spiritual retreat methodologies will yield an incredible deepening of communal bonds. We are increasingly recommending that people take smaller retreats for intimate-sized community groups (two to five people) and table-sized community groups (eight to twelve people). We recommend prayer retreats, spiritual discipline retreats, topically oriented equipping retreats, and even retreats just for the sake of communal enjoyment (to rest and have fun). Each allows people to step out of their context and begin taking a more meta (broad perspective) approach to their lives. Each kind of retreat also allows people the time to create a "speech act" to themselves concerning their level of commitment to pursuing the Lord.[16]

Retreats can be some of the most powerful and life-changing experiences for individuals and entire communities. A good friend of ours had a community that went on quarterly spiritual retreats. He said that retreat and deep community became the norm for them. Everything else in between was just building on the depth that they had created in their culture together.

Missions trips: We have seen countless lives infinitely impacted by going on missions trips. Jeremy's entire life trajectory is the result of a missions trip in 1999 to La Plata, Argentina. After a one-week trip where he was exposed to the missional movement of the Holy Spirit, Jeremy saw part of his identity as a "sent person." It was through that experience that he touched on the eternal work of God, and it transformed him. It only took three days before he knew that his entire life direction had changed and that a component of his greater purpose in life had been revealed to him. His dad, Tom, went along with him on the trip, and Tom's entire ministry shifted direction as well. In one week, they saw entire households repent in tears, streets become new church plants, and a harvest of epic proportions. The fruit continued for years, not only in their lives but also in the lives of many of those living in that area.

Through the fifty-plus missions trips we have since taken (both globally and to the US), we have seen almost every trip yield some level of change in life direction for people. If a missional community,

---

[16] A speech act is an action that speaks loudly and communicates more than what is understood at mere face value. For example, marriage is a speech act of great magnitude—to marry someone says *much more* about aspects of the relationship than merely saying that you love them. Another speech act is a tattoo—it typically says much more than the mere visual aspect. In the context of retreats then, a spiritual retreat is a speech act to oneself, demonstrating one's own willingness to take the time, energy, and resources to place priority on intimacy with Jesus. It says more than we fully know, and the true depth of this action can take quite some time to fully unpack. *Gravitas* by Jerome Daley is an excellent read that helps demonstrate the true nature of our speech acts when we practice spiritual formation.

a Sunday school group, a small group, or a microchurch decides to enter into an apostolic mission, they will see the beginnings of deep community.

Risk: The same can be said of undertaking various endeavors with large faith-stretching goals—taking on the seemingly impossible for the sake of seeing God glorified by overcoming our human limitations to achieve mind-blowing results. Taking risks will bring us to the end of ourselves, and our dependence on God will escalate to 100 percent. These are times when individuals and communities of believers experience the reality of full God-dependence for movement forward—when *only God* can make it happen. We need to open ourselves up to the adventures that are available when we leave our sanitized, artificial environments that promote safety and a clone mentality.

Even if a small group goes on a day trip, a road trip, or just begins to explore life in more experimental ways, adventure, risk, and faith-stretching each become something significant. This can expand to include business endeavors or projects within your city to serve in various ways. The same goes for covenants that result in deepening commitments toward one another. When we commit to care, confront with love, give, receive, and walk alongside those who are hurting, we will see greater depth in our community. This place of risk is where we test the strength of our faith, our relationships, and our willingness to sacrifice and trust God.

Tool #6: A Week in the Life...

In Caesar Kalinowski's excellent work *Small Is Big, Slow Is Fast*, he describes a week in the life of a missional practitioner.[17] We have adapted this for our purposes here. Let's consider a typical week in the life of a Trinitarian/Jesus-centered/missional/incarnational/

---

[17] Caesar Kalinowski, *Small is Big, Slow is Fast: Living and Leading Your Family and Community on God's Mission* (Zondervan, 2014), chapter eight.

movemental/discipling practitioner (what a mouthful!). This could include the following elements and dynamics:

- Enough margin to be able to intentionally love those around you and embrace interruptions in your schedule as potential divine appointments
- Sufficient time with the Lord to be contemplative, still in his presence, and growing in intimacy with him
- A few meals with people
- Thinking about your workplace intentionally as a mission field
- Intentional connections with neighbors or certain people groups in the city
- Participation in an intimate space of micro-communal discipleship
- Involvement in various small-group spaces
- Participation in party spaces
- Living out the values of SEARCH (mentioned in chapter two on discipleship)

If you don't yet have a group to meet with, see the guidelines in the appendix, "How to Start a Microchurch," at the end of this book.

IT'S SCRIPTURAL. IT'S RATIONAL. IT'S TRANSFORMATIONAL.

Of course!

AFTERWORD

Alan Hirsch

There are books that make a contribution. Then there are books that become companions on the journey—maps, even, for those daring enough to join the adventure of God's kingdom. *Kingdom Contours* is that kind of book. Now that you've walked through its pages, you know this isn't just theory—it's field-tested, Spirit-breathed wisdom. In Jeremy and Monica Chambers, we have two seasoned practitioners who don't just write about movement—they embody it. These two are the real deal—faithful friends and fellow travelers in the work of gospel movement. They've dared to ask the hard questions, risk the slow answers, and live out the kind of Jesus-centered, Spirit-fueled life that most only dream of.

What they've laid out here is more than a manual. It's a summons. Drawing from deep wells of biblical theology, global experience, and contemplative practice, *Kingdom Contours* offers a toolbelt for catalyzing real, transformative disciple-making movements. It reflects the DNA of movements throughout history—what I've called the mDNA—and translates it into clear, accessible pathways for everyday people. This book stands as a practical elaboration of the six elements I first outlined in *The Forgotten Ways*. Jeremy and Monica take that movement theory and breathe life into it with grounded insight, stories from the edge, and tools forged in practice. They give shape to what might otherwise remain distant or abstract.

The kingdom doesn't advance through spectators. It moves with the faithful, the risk-takers, the lovers of Jesus who say "yes" to his wild and beautiful way. Welcome to the adventure—now go live it.

ACKNOWLEDGMENTS

It takes a team to create a book of this quality, and certainly, we have seen the quality elevated over and over again by a large number of people who helped us in this process.

First, thank you, Father, for your wisdom and love to us in creating us and inviting us into your cosmic-level hug. Thank you, Jesus, for loving us and having such a wise, gentle, and humble perspective; and for your vision of the joy that was ahead, which meant you endured the cross to bring about a better reality for us all. It brings tears to our eyes to consider that! Thank you, Spirit, for being the Great Comforter, encircling us, abiding within us, and being the very Light of God to us—guiding and revealing just what we needed at the right time. Your intimacy is infinitely deep and worth giving the entirety of our lives to. Thank you, Trinity, for being incomprehensibly Trinitarian because you are sheer beauty beyond what our minds can comprehend.

Second, thank you to our parents, teachers, theology professors, mentors, coaches, friends, supporters, and ministry partners (via all the various ministries from over the years). You have helped to shape and encourage us along the way. It should be noted that our parents were also our teachers, theology professors, mentors, coaches, friends, supporters, and ministry partners ... so they get extra thanks for being in every one of those categories! Uncle John: thanks for Rony.

Jeremy thanks Monica, and Monica thanks Jeremy. (Imagine us doing a fist pound at this moment, saying "thanks" to one another.)

And special "chronological" thanks go to the following for making this project excellent.

2017–2019: "THE ARISE BLUEPRINT" (ORIGINAL MANUSCRIPT)

Liz Desmarais, for taking the initial manuscript and doing our first-ever proof (and for removing those eighty-seven million parentheticals).

Wendell Globig, for working with us on brevity. Alan Hirsch, for encouraging us to take the manuscript to the next level: You have been with us through this entire writing journey, and this book would never have even been published the first time if it wasn't for your encouragement.

Thank you to all the beta readers, the Arise people (all of you who endured the original version and continued loving us as we went through burnout around that time). Thanks to all the additional proofreaders and those who offered great feedback in improving the original manuscript—there are too many people to name here. Sam Mahisekar offered great encouragement and support by taking our writing to the next level. Sam, you also planted the seeds that led to us writing *The Art of Missional Spirituality* later on!

We thank the Lord for guiding us through human and spiritual opposition and trials that helped to create the first manuscript. He redeemed the attacks and what others had meant for harm to settle us more firmly in our convictions and calling, which had an overwhelming influence on the creation of this book. God redeems 100 percent!

2020: KINGDOM CONTOURS (INITIAL PUBLICATION)

Russ Johnson, for pushing us forward to get the original version published with Dave Devries at Missional Challenge Publishing. Thank you also, Dave, for all your theological editing during the process. Thanks to Tony Sorci for the original cover and brainstorming. Rachael Grotte, for editing the first edition and working wonders—you had some heavy lifting to do and handled it with grace. Terry Ishee, for being a total champion of us and our book; we won't forget your support.

2025: KINGDOM CONTOURS (REVISED PUBLICATION)

Brenna Varner, remember that moment when Jeremy was struggling with paralyzing fear and you spoke a powerful truth into his life? That empowered him and brought him freedom. This revised version has become a reality because of how the Lord used you in that moment. Thank you. Brenna and Joel, thank you for your friendship, partnership, and all the work you have done to help bring both books into reality and to get the word out! Thank you also for loving your neighbors as much as you do.

Anna and Rich Robinson, thank you for your friendship, hospitality, and all the work that you do to make Movement Leaders Collective and 100 Movements Publishing thrive. Anna, thank you for the miracles you have done in taking this manuscript to the next level, and for just being so cool! You inspire us. Thank you also for loving your city as much as you do: Jesus is using you there.

Helen Bearn: Well, well, well …. we meet again in the acknowledgments of another book. Your approach to editing has encouraged, empowered, and even equipped us in our lives. (It is just an accident that all those words started with "e.") We cannot possibly express our gratitude with words, but thank you for your commitment to excellence. You, Jon, and your children are so awesome. Thank you for your love for the body of Christ and for your local missional community.

Thank you to all the endorsers and Amazon "reviewers"!

Thanks once again, Alan and Deb Hirsch, for all your support and generosity along the way.

Thank you, Mike Frost, for writing such an impressive foreword! Wow! Thank you also for your heart of generosity and kindness.

Thank you especially to the people in Forge and Renováre for all the help, support, partnership, reinforcement, and love over the years! Your relational investment in us has helped shape us and has made the book even better.

APPENDIX

How to Start a Microchurch

1. Gather with at least one person for weekly prayer. As you pray, seek the Lord concerning the mission needs in your area and the people group that he is calling you to serve. Ask him to raise up laborers; ask him to reveal how you can begin taking small steps toward reaching the lost; ask how he wants you to be going deeper together as followers of Jesus. Let every group start with prayer!

2. When the time is right (and you must discern this), begin reading some Scriptures together on a weekly basis. Ask "What? How? Who?" as you look at the text:
    - *What* has God highlighted to you in his Word (deeper listening to his voice)?
    - *How* will you obey (learning to obey God by grace, together)?
    - *Who* is God putting on your heart to reach (going into his mission)?

3. After a few months, take time to reflect and decide if you want to commit to continuing these practices or if the Lord is leading you to stop. Every group needs an opportunity to shut down. If it isn't right, it shouldn't continue; but if the Lord is doing a good work in you and those you are meeting with, you will want to count the cost together before going forward. Set an appointed time in the future to revisit these things again.

4. If the group continues, pray together about others who can join you in your mission; but call them to the mission clearly and help them understand what they are committing to. This is a time when you don't want to bring in just anyone. You want to ask people who are willing to make sacrifices to serve

alongside you, and you want to ask those who are FATO (faithful, available, teachable, and operational).

5. As a small team forms (usually two to five people), begin discovering people's APEST gifts and discern how the team can start operating according to these. Make sure to incorporate APEST rhythms into your monthly rhythm. Don't let too much time go by without doing something apostolic, prophetic, evangelistic, shepherding, and teaching for the group. If you don't incorporate these APEST rhythms at the beginning, you will begin to shape the group according to the common giftings of the leaders, rather than allowing the fullness of the body to be expressed.

6. At some point (when the group reaches between eight and twelve people), it will be time to follow one of these options:
   o Multiply by sending two or three out.
   o Multiply by splitting the group up. (Often, people don't want this as it can be relationally challenging.)
   o Close the group for a period of time to go deeper, but do not lose sight of the need to eventually plant a new group.
   o Keep getting bigger and change your structure accordingly. (We don't recommend this last option unless you have adequate resources to make this shift. Bear in mind, it is also a move away from the vision and intention of the microchurch.)

RECOMMENDED RESOURCES

CLASSICS

- *Conformed to His Image: Biblical and Practical Approaches to Spiritual Formation*, by Kenneth Boa[1]
- *Center Church: Doing Balanced, Gospel-Centered Ministry in Your City*, by Timothy Keller[2]
- *The ESV Study Bible*[3]
- *The Gospel Primer*, by Caesar Kalinowski
- *Living Free in Christ: The Truth About Who You Are and How Christ Can Meet Your Deepest Needs*, by Neil T. Anderson[4]
- *Mere Christianity*, by C. S. Lewis
- *Institutes of the Christian Religion*, by John Calvin[5]
- *The Confessions*, by St. Augustine
- *According to Plan: The Unfolding Revelation of God in the Bible*, by Graeme Goldsworthy[6]

---

[1] This book addresses twelve aspects of spiritual formation/growth. This is a library in a book.

[2] Also a library in a book, this book 1) masterfully defines the gospel and its application to many aspects of life, 2) identifies God's heart for nations and cities, 3) resourcefully addresses contextualization, and 4) provides a theological framework for understanding the church on mission.

[3] This is a scholarly yet accessible study Bible. The articles address an incredible range of topics: biblical ethics, systematic theology, world religions, philosophy of religion, Bible background issues, and much more.

[4] This book examines identity in Christ and is a resource for equipping people for personal breakthroughs.

[5] Despite some people disliking "modern Calvinism," this book is a worshipful, classic piece of theology that will bless people on both sides of the debate and unpack a refreshing dose of theological perspective.

[6] Responding to the over-systematization of theology, Goldsworthy provides a decisive move toward unifying theology under the natural narratives and themes that tie all of Scripture into

GOD THE FATHER

- *Knowing God,* by J. I. Packer
- *The Reason for God: Belief in an Age of Skepticism,* by Timothy Keller
- *The Good and Beautiful God: Falling in Love with the God Jesus Knows,* by James Bryan Smith
- *A Beam of Divine Glory: The Unchangeableness of God,* by Edward Pearse[7]
- *God's Passion for His Glory: Living the Vision of Jonathan Edwards,* by John Piper[8]
- *To Love as God Loves: Conversations with the Early Church,* by Roberta Bondi[9]

JESUS

- *Jesus Christ Our Lord,* by John Walvoord
- *Seeing and Savoring Jesus Christ,* by John Piper

HOLY SPIRIT

- *He Who Gives Life: The Doctrine of the Holy Spirit,* by Graham Cole[10]
- *Power Evangelism,* by John Wimber[11]

---

a cohesive whole. If you have never read any treatment of "biblical theology" as such, this is a perfect starting point and essential to a better understanding of the Scriptures.

[7] This excellent Puritan work will expand your worship and imagination with respect to God's power and majesty.

[8] This is two books in one: Jonathan Edwards's *The End for which God Created the World* with John Piper's commentary. It is unbelievably powerful and stretching for any reader seeking to know the Triune Godhead more deeply than before.

[9] Bondi examines the desert fathers and mothers and distills their perspective of the Triune God, love, and humility.

[10] A comprehensive, humble, and refreshing theological and historical perspective on the Holy Spirit.

[11] This book reflects current phenomena in global missiology regarding the supernatural activity of the Holy Spirit. Wimber's understanding of church history and his willingness to be rational

MISSIOLOGY/CHURCH MATTERS/DISCIPLESHIP

- *The Forgotten Ways: Reactivating Apostolic Movements,* by Alan Hirsch
- *Small is Big, Slow is Fast: Living and Leading Your Family and Community on God's Mission,* by Caesar Kalinowski[12]
- *Cross-Cultural Servanthood: Serving the World in Christlike Humility,* by Duane Elmer
- *The Complete Book of Discipleship: On Being and Making Followers of Christ,* by Bill Hull
- *Disciplism: Reimagining Evangelism Through the Lens of Discipleship,* by Alan Hirsch
- *I Once Was Lost: What Postmodern Skeptics Taught Us About Their Path to Jesus,* by Don Everts and Doug Schaupp[13]
- *The Celtic Way of Evangelism: How Christianity Can Reach the West ... AGAIN,* by George C. Hunter[14]
- *Marketplace Christianity: Discovering the Kingdom Purpose of the Marketplace,* by Robert Fraser
- *The Permanent Revolution: Apostolic Imagination and Practice for the 21st Century Church,* by Alan Hirsch and Tim Catchim[15]
- *The Tangible Kingdom Primer: An Eight-Week Guide to Incarnational Community,* by Hugh Halter and Matt Smay[16]
- *The Master Plan of Evangelism,* by Dr. Robert E. Coleman

---

while examining the work of the Holy Spirit makes this a healthy read even for those who disagree with much of the book.

[12] A solid application of the missional/incarnational and organic lifestyle. This is one of the best books on these topics (especially for families looking to live incarnationally).

[13] This book identifies the thresholds people move through while coming to a place of faith in Christ.

[14] A book to fuel practical theory about how to create missional communities that are effectively incarnational and contextualized to their environments.

[15] Centered around explaining the five gifts (apostle, prophet, evangelist, shepherd, teacher) mentioned in Ephesians 4, with a special focus on apostle/pioneer. This is one of Jeremy's all-time favorite books.

[16] An excellent workbook for individuals or groups who are seeking to be missional and incarnational.

- *A Meal with Jesus: Discovering Grace, Community, and Mission around the Table,* by Tim Chester
- *Perspectives on the World Christian Movement: A Reader,* 4th ed., edited by Ralph D. Winter and Steven C. Hawthorne
- *Let the Nations Be Glad! The Supremacy of God in Missions,* by John Piper
- *From Jerusalem to Iryan Jaya: A Biographical History of Christian Missions,* by Ruth Tucker[17]

SERVANTHOOD/LEADERSHIP

- *Leadership as an Identity: The Four Traits of Those Who Wield Lasting Influence,* by Crawford W. Loritts[18]
- *The Contemplative Pastor: Returning to the Art of Spiritual Direction,* by Eugene Peterson[19]
- *Visioneering: Your Guide for Discovering and Maintaining Personal Vision,* by Andy Stanley
- *Developing the Leaders Around You: How to Help Others Reach Their Full Potential,* by John Maxwell
- *Equipping 101,* by John Maxwell
- *Good Leaders Ask Great Questions: Your Foundation for Successful Leadership,* by John Maxwell
- *The Making of a Leader: Recognizing the Lessons and Stages of Leadership Development,* by Dr. J. Robert Clinton

BIBLICAL INTERPRETATION

- *How to Read the Bible for All Its Worth,* by Gordon D. Fee and Douglas Stuart
- *Dictionary for Theological Interpretation of the Bible,* by Kevin J. Vanhoozer (general editor)[20]

---

[17] Detailing missions history from a realistic, raw, unexaggerated, and inspirational perspective.

[18] One of the best books on spiritual leadership.

[19] A must-read for spiritual leaders as they consider their calling and those they are ministering to.

[20] This book gives an incredibly insightful approach to a range of theological perspectives.

- *The Dictionary of Major Bible Interpreters,* edited by Donald K. McKim[21]
- *Exegetical Fallacies,* by D. A. Carson[22]

GENERAL THEOLOGICAL READS

- *The Beatitudes: An Exposition of Matthew 5:1–12,* by Thomas Watson[23]
- *A Jonathan Edwards Reader,* edited by John E. Smith, Harry S. Stout, and Kenneth P. Minkema
- *The Sermons of Jonathan Edwards: A Reader,* edited by Wilson H. Kimnach, Kenneth P. Minkema, and Douglas A. Sweeney
- *Renovation of the Heart: Putting on the Character of Christ,* by Dallas Willard
- *The Divine Conspiracy: Rediscovering Our Hidden Life in God,* by Dallas Willard[24]
- *Created in God's Image,* by Anthony Hoekema
- *Not The Way It's Supposed to Be: A Breviary of Sin,* by Cornelius Plantinga Jr.
- *Keep Christianity Weird: Embracing the Discipline of Being Different,* by Michael Frost[25]
- *Deeper Experiences of Famous Christians,* by James Gilchrist Lawson[26]

---

[21] This book is a comprehensive treatment of various approaches to interpreting Scripture throughout church history. For advanced study.

[22] This book is for those who really want to go deeper to avoid fallacies and poor interpretive work. If you plan on doing extensive Bible teaching/interpreting/application in your ministry, this is a must-read.

[23] A masterful Puritan treatment of the Beatitudes.

[24] On God's master plan and how we fit into it and can participate in his kingdom.

[25] One of Frost's best books, it is concise but shares great insights into the history of Christianity with nuances that many historians overlook or omit.

[26] The abridged version offers a glimpse into the historically significant and unique experiences of impactful Christians.

SPIRITUAL FORMATION

- *Sacred Pathways: Discover Your Soul's Path to God*, by Gary Thomas
- *The Spirit of the Disciplines: Understanding How God Changes Lives*, by Dallas Willard
- *Spiritual Disciplines Handbook: Practices That Transform Us*, by Adele Calhoun
- *Celebration of Discipline: The Path to Spiritual Growth*, by Richard Foster
- *Ruthless Trust: The Ragamuffin's Path to God*, by Brennan Manning
- *Abba's Child: The Cry of the Heart for Intimate Belonging*, by Brennan Manning
- *The Art of Missional Spirituality: 31 Sacred Practices for Jesus-Followers*, by Jeremy Chambers and Monica Paredes Chambers
- *The Rest of God: Restoring Your Soul by Restoring Sabbath*, by Mark Buchanan[27]

GENERAL CHRISTIAN LIVING/ISSUES

- *For a Time We Cannot See: Living Today in Light of Heaven*, by Crawford Loritts
- *The Myth Of Equality: Uncovering the Roots of Injustice and Privilege*, by Ken Wytsma[28]
- *A Tapestry of Faiths: The Common Threads Between Christianity and World Religions*, by Winfried Corduan[29]
- *Encouragement: The Unexpected Power of Building Others Up*, by Dan B. Allender and Larry J. Crabb Jr.
- *The 5 Apology Languages: The Secret to Healthy Relationships*, by Gary Chapman and Jennifer Thomas

---

[27] An excellent book on sabbath rest.

[28] An insightful book on how the church should view race-related tensions, specifically in the US.

[29] On understanding and replying to religious pluralism.

- *Redeeming Sex: Naked Conversations About Sexuality and Spirituality,* by Debra Hirsch[30]
- *Bringing Sex Into Focus: The Quest for Sexual Integrity,* by Caroline J. Simon[31]
- *Heaven: A Comprehensive Guide to Everything the Bible Says About Our Eternal Home,* by Randy Alcorn
- *Boundaries: When to Say Yes, How to Say No to Take Control of Your Life,* by Dr. Henry Cloud and Dr. John Townsend[32]
- *A Grief Observed,* by C. S. Lewis
- *Walking with God through Pain and Suffering,* by Timothy Keller
- *The Problem of Pain,* by C. S. Lewis
- *The Great Divorce,* by C. S. Lewis
- *The Four Loves,* by C. S. Lewis
- *The Screwtape Letters,* by C. S. Lewis
- *Failure: The Back Door to Success,* by Erwin Lutzer
- *Everyday Theology: How to Read Cultural Text and Interpret Trends,* edited by Kevin J. Vanhoozer, Charles A. Anderson, and Michael J. Sleasman[33]
- *The Peacemaker: A Biblical Guide to Resolving Personal Conflict,* by Ken Sande[34]
- *Inside Out,* by Dr. Larry Crabb[35]
- *When Helping Hurts: How to Alleviate Poverty Without Hurting the Poor … and Yourself,* by Steve Corbett and Brian Fikkert
- *The Hole In Our Gospel: What Does God Expect of Us? The Answer*

---

[30] Contains excellent and challenging understandings of sexuality and gender. Many Christians still make assumptions that are not biblically based. Hirsch focuses on unearthing some of those assumptions and pointing us toward loving and Christlike awareness of where people are at, without compromising on what is truly biblical.

[31] On Christian sexual ethics. This book details six lenses that people use to understand sexuality. Simon talks about how to keep these lenses in their appropriate places concerning the biblical unifying ethical perspective on sex.

[32] Everyone should read this book to understand how to appropriately protect themselves in order to minister to others without burning out or enabling codependent behavior in others.

[33] On reading and understanding cultural texts.

[34] On conflict resolution.

[35] On understanding heart motivations.

That Changed My Life and Might Just Change the World, by Richard Stearns[36]

- *The Principle of The Path: How to Get from Where You Are to Where You Want to Be,* by Andy Stanley[37]

PRAYER

- *Praying with Paul: A Call to Spiritual Reformation,* by D. A. Carson
- *Fresh Wind, Fresh Fire: What Happens When God's Spirit Invades the Hearts of His People,* by Jim Cymbala with Dean Merrill
- *Providence and Prayer: How Does God Work in the World?,* by Terrance Tiessen[38]
- *The Practice of the Presence of God,* by Brother Lawrence
- *Intimacy with the Almighty,* by Charles R. Swindoll
- *A Guide for Listening and Inner-Healing Prayer: Meeting God in the Broken Places,* by Rusty Rustenbach[39]
- *Prayer: Finding the Heart's True Home,* by Richard Foster
- *Hearing God: Developing a Conversational Relationship with God,* by Dallas Willard[40]

MISCELLANEOUS

- *The Compound Effect: Multiply Your Success One Simple Step at a Time,* by Darren Hardy
- *The Freedom of Self-Forgetfulness: The Path to True Christian Joy,* by Timothy Keller
- *The Orthodox Way,* by Kallistos Ware[41]

---

[36] On a more holistic gospel that cares for the poor.

[37] On the natural compounding effect of decisions in our lives. This book frees us up to consider how our current lifestyle and decisions can easily impact our future in incredible ways (both positive and negative).

[38] This book demonstrates how our theology impacts our prayers and offers ten models for creating consistency between our theological awareness and prayer practices.

[39] A biblically based approach for applying truth to areas of internal lies and pain.

[40] A balanced approach to a tricky topic.

[41] The Orthodox church brings incredible insights into the Trinity and life and practice of faith.

- *The Tipping Point: How Little Things Can Make a Big Difference,* by Malcolm Gladwell
- *Unseen: The Gift of Being Hidden in a World That Loves to Be Noticed,* by Sara Hagerty[42]
- *Life in the Trinity: an Introduction to Theology with the Help of the Church Fathers,* by Donald Fairbairn[43]
- *New Dictionary of Biblical Theology,* edited by T. Desmond Alexander, Brian S. Rosner, D. A. Carson, and Graeme Goldsworthy
- *The Scandal of Leadership: Unmasking the Powers of Domination in the Church,* by JR Woodward[44]

---

[42] Excellent insights regarding ministry as true worship unto the Lord, not for the praise or acknowledgment of people.

[43] An excellent resource on Johannine theology and the early church fathers' application of the idea of "union with Christ" as being central to the Christian faith.

[44] An excellent resource on spiritual warfare from a robust and healthy academic with applied perspective.

RECOMMENDED ORGANIZATIONS TO CONNECT WITH

We personally recommend and have greatly benefited from the work of two organizations: Forge and Renovaré.

Forge America is an organization of kingdom-oriented people participating in the mission of God. This network of missional practitioners cultivates others to follow Jesus in his everyday mission, equipping them to be sent in the same way he was sent. Forge America invites individuals to join its community, which offers mutual support, curates conversation, and provides training and resources for living a missional life. To learn more about Forge America, please visit www.ForgeAmerica.com and fill out the connection form on the website. Alternatively, inquiries can be sent via info@forgeamerica.com.

Renovaré is a ministry and community that models, resources, and advocates fullness of life with God experienced, by grace, through the spiritual practices of Jesus and of the historical church. They are Christian in commitment, ecumenical in breadth, and international in scope. Renovaré helps people become more like Jesus. They offer a variety of means (a two-year institute, conferences, retreats, book club, prayer groups, and church renewal cohorts) to equip people to walk with Jesus and become more like Jesus. They are the real deal. You can find out more at: www.renovare.org.

BIBLIOGRAPHY

Anderson, Neil T. *Living Free in Christ: The Truth About Who You Are and How Christ Can Meet Your Deepest Needs*. Regal Books, 1993.

Boa, Kenneth. *Conformed to His Image: Biblical and Practical Approaches to Spiritual Formation*. Zondervan, 2001.

Bonhoeffer, Dietrich. *Life Together: The Classic Exploration of Faith in Community*. 5th ed. HarperSanFrancisco, 2009.

Bosch, David. *Transforming Mission: Paradigm Shifts in Theology of Mission*. Orbis Books, 1991.

Buchanan, Mark. *The Rest of God: Restoring Your Soul by Restoring Sabbath*. Thomas Nelson, 2006.

Butler, Phill. *Well Connected: Releasing Power, Restoring Hope Through Kingdom Partnerships*. Authentic Media, 2006.

Carson, D. A. *Praying with Paul: A Call to Spiritual Reformation*. 2nd ed. Baker Academic, 2015.

Chambers, Jeremy. "The Mechanics and Spirituality of Trust." V3. Accessed April 25, 2025. http://thev3movement.org/2019/04/16/the-mechanics-and-spirituality-of-trust/.

Chambers, Jeremy, and Monica Paredes Chambers. *The Art of Missional Spirituality: 31 Sacred Practices for Jesus-Followers*. 100 Movements Publishing, 2023.

Clinton, Dr. J. Robert. *The Making of a Leader: Recognizing the Lessons and Stages of Leadership Development*. 2nd ed. NavPress, 2012.

Cloud, Dr. Henry, and Dr. John Townsend. *Boundaries: When to Say Yes, How to Say No to Take Control of Your Life*. Updated and revised ed. Zondervan. 2017.

Cole, Neil. *Organic Church: Growing Faith Where Life Happens*. Jossey-Bass, 2005.

Coleman, Dr. Robert E. *The Master Plan of Evangelism*. Revell, 1994.

Corbett, Steve, and Brian Fikkert. *When Helping Hurts: How to Alleviate Poverty Without Hurting the Poor... and Yourself*. Moody, 2012.

Crabb, Larry. *The Safest Place on Earth: Where People Connect and Are Forever Changed*. W Pub Group, 1999.

Daley, Jerome. *Gravitas: The Monastic Rhythms of Healthy Leadership*. NavPress, 2020.

Edwards, Jonathan. *The End for Which God Created the World*. CreateSpace Publishing, 2014.

Elmer, Duane. *Cross-Cultural Connections: Stepping Out and Fitting in Around the World*. InterVarsity Press, 2002.

Everts, Don, and Doug Schaupp. *I Once Was Lost: What Postmodern Skeptics Taught Us About Their Path to Jesus*. InterVarsity Press, 2008.

Fairbairn, Donald. *Life in the Trinity: An Introduction to Theology with the Help of the Church Fathers*. InterVarsity Press, 2009.

Foster, Richard. *Streams of Living Water: Celebrating the Great Traditions of Christian Faith*. Hodder and Stoughton, 2019.

Fraser, Robert. *Marketplace Christianity: Discovering the Kingdom Purpose of the Marketplace*. New Grid Books, 2011.

Frost, Michael. *Surprise the World: The Five Habits of Highly Missional People*. NavPress, 2015.

Frost, Michael, and Alan Hirsch. *The Faith of Leap: Embracing a Theology of Risk, Adventure and Courage*, revised ed. 100 Movements Publishing, 2025.

Frost, Michael, and Christina Rice. *To Alter Your World: Partnering with God to Rebirth Our Communities*. InterVarsity Press, 2017.

Garrison, David. *Church Planting Movements: How God is Redeeming a Lost World*. Wigtake Resources, 2003.

Gladwell, Malcolm. *The Tipping Point: How Little Things Can Make a Big Difference*. Little, Brown and Company, 2000.

Grieg, Pete, and Dave Roberts. *Red Moon Rising: Rediscover the Power of Prayer*. David C. Cook, 2015.

Grudem, Wayne. *The Gift of Prophecy in the New Testament and Today*. Crossway, 2000.

Hagberg, Janet O., and Robert A. Guelich. *The Critical Journey: Stages in the Life of Faith*. Sheffield Publishing Company, 2005.

Hall, Edward T. *The Hidden Dimension*. Bantam Doubleday, 1988.

Halter, Hugh, and Matt Smay. *The Tangible Kingdom Primer: An Eight-Week Guide to Incarnational Community*. Missio Publishing, 2009.

Halter, Hugh, and Matt Smay. *The Tangible Kingdom: Creating Incarnational Community*. Jossey-Bass, 2008.

Hardy, Darren. *The Compound Effect: Multiply Your Success One Simple Step at a Time*. Vanguard Press, 2010.

Heath, Dan, and Chip Heath. *Made to Stick: Why Some Ideas Take Hold and Others Come Unstuck*. Arrow, 2008.

Hirsch, Alan. *Disciplism: Reimagining Evangelism Through the Lens of Discipleship*. 100 Movements Publishing, 2023.

Hirsch, Alan. *The Forgotten Ways: Reactivating the Missional Church*. Brazos Press, 2009.

Hirsch, Alan. *5Q: Reactivating the Original Intelligence and Capacity of the Body of Christ*. 100 Movements Publishing, 2017.

Hirsch, Alan, and Tim Catchim. *The Permanent Revolution: Apostolic Imagination and Practice for the 21st Century Church*. Jossey-Bass, 2012.

Hull, Bill. *The Complete Book of Discipleship: On Being and Making Followers of Christ*. NavPress, 2006.

Hunter, George C. *The Celtic Way of Evangelism: How Christianity Can Reach the West ... AGAIN*, 10th ed. Abingdon Press, 2011.

Johnson, Russ, and Tony Sorci. *Reclaim: Reclaiming the Church's Identity and Ministry as a Liberated People of Indiscriminate Grace*. Independently published, 2021.

Kalinowski, Caesar. *The Gospel Primer*. Missio Publishing, 2012.

Kalinowski, Caesar. *Small is Big, Slow is Fast: Living and Leading Your Family and Community on God's Mission*. Zondervan, 2014.

Keller, Timothy. *Center Church: Doing Balanced, Gospel-Centered Ministry in Your City*. Zondervan, 2012.

Keller, Timothy. *The Freedom of Self-Forgetfulness: The Path to True Christian Joy*. 10Publishing, 2012.

Lewis, C. S. *The Four Loves*. HarperOne, 2017.

Lewis, C. S. *The Screwtape Letters*. HarperOne, 2015.

Loritts, Crawford W. *Leadership as an Identity: The Four Traits of Those Who Wield Lasting Influence*. Moody, 2009.

Manning, Brennan. *Abba's Child: The Cry of the Heart for Intimate Belonging*. NavPress, 2015.

Navidi, Sandra. *SuperHubs: How the Financial Elite and Their Networks Rule Our World*. Nicholas Brealey Publishing, 2017.

Nouwen, Henri. *In the Name of Jesus: Reflections on Christian Leadership*. Darton, Longman and Todd Ltd., 1989.

Packer, J. I. *Evangelism and the Sovereignty of God*. InterVarsity Press, 2012.

Packer, J. I. *Knowing God*, 3rd ed. Hodder and Stroughton, 2005.

Peterson, Eugene. *The Contemplative Pastor: Returning to the Art of Spiritual Direction*. Baker, 2004.

Piper, John. *God's Passion for His Glory: Living the Vision of Jonathan Edwards*. Crossway, 2006.

Roxburgh, Alan J. *Missional: Joining God in the Neighborhood*. Baker, 2011.

Sande, Ken. *The Peacemaker: A Biblical Guide to Resolving Personal Conflict*. Baker, 2004.

Scott, Susan. *Fierce Conversations: Achieving Success in Work and in Life, One Conversation at a Time*. Piatkus, 2017.

Sellers, Jeff. "Church closures, attacks spike worldwide, WWL 2024 reports." *Christian Daily International*, January 17, 2024, https://www.christiandaily.com/news/church-closures-attacks-spike-worldwide-wwl-2024-reports.

Smith, James Bryan. *The Good and Beautiful God: Falling in Love with the God Jesus Knows*. InterVarsity Press, 2009.

Stanley, Andy. *The Principle of the Path: How to Get from Where You Are to Where You Want to Be*. Thomas Nelson, 2011.

Stearns, Richard. *The Hole In Our Gospel: What Does God Expect of Us? The Answer That Changed My Life and Might Just Change the World*. Thomas Nelson, 2014.

Stone, Douglas, Bruce Patton, Sheila Heen, and Roger Fisher. *Difficult Conversations: How to Discuss What Matters Most*. 10th anniversary ed. Penguin, 1990.

Stott, John. *The Message of Ephesians: God's New Society.* 3rd ed. InterVarsity Press, 1991.

Thomas, Gary. *Sacred Pathways: Discover Your Soul's Path to God.* Zondervan, 2000.

Tiessen, Terrance. *Providence and Prayer: How Does God Work in the World?* IVP Academic, 2000.

Trebesch, Shelley G. *Isolation: A Place of Transformation In The Life of a Leader.* Barnabas Publishing, 1997.

Tuckman, Bruce. "Developmental Sequence in Small Groups." *Psychological Bulletin* 63(6), 1965.

Vanderstelt, Jeff. *Gospel Fluency: Speaking the Truths of Jesus into the Everyday Stuff of Life.* Crossway, 2017.

Vanhoozer, Kevin J., Charles A. Anderson, and Michael J. Sleasman, eds. *Everyday Theology: How to Read Cultural Texts and Interpret Trends.* Baker Academic, 2007.

Viola, Frank. *Reimagining Church: Pursuing the Dream of Organic Christianity.* David C. Cook, 2008.

Willard, Dallas. *The Divine Conspiracy: Rediscovering Our Hidden Life in God.* HarperCollins, 1998.

Willard, Dallas. *Renovation of the Heart: Putting on the Character of Christ.* NavPress, 2002.

Wimber, John. *Power Evangelism.* Chosen Books, 1986.

Winter, Ralph. "The High Priority: Cross-Cultural Evangelism." *Perspectives on the World Christian Movement.* 4th ed. William Carey Publishing, 2009.

Woodward, JR. *Creating a Missional Culture: Equipping the Church for the Sake of the World.* InterVarsity Press, 2012.

Woodward, JR, and Dan White Jr. *The Church as Movement: Starting and Sustaining Missional-Incarnational Communities.* InterVarsity Press, 2016.

Wright, N. T. *Paul for Everyone: The Prison Letters.* SPCK Publishing, 2002.

Voskamp, Ann. *One Thousand Gifts: A Dare to Live Fully Right Where You Are.* Thomas Nelson, 2011.

ABOUT THE AUTHORS

JEREMY AND MONICA CHAMBERS have participated in launching movements that make disciples and networks of microchurches in over thirty-five countries. They currently practice incarnational mission as they develop discipling missional communities in Denver, Colorado, and the broader region. They are partnered with Forge America (to provide missional resourcing) and Renovaré (with a focus on spiritual formation).

Jeremy earned his BA in Bible at Lancaster Bible College, an MA in intercultural studies, and an MA in history of Christian thought/church history at Trinity Evangelical Divinity School. He also has his black belt in multiple martial arts.

Monica is Costa Rican but came to the US with her parents as missionaries. She took Christian studies at Columbia International University and graphic design at The Art Institute of York. She is a personal trainer and fitness instructor.

Jeremy and Monica love rock climbing, hiking, reading, and heavy metal. They previously authored *The Art of Missional Spirituality: 31 Sacred Practices for Jesus-Followers.*

ALSO BY JEREMY AND MONICA CHAMBERS

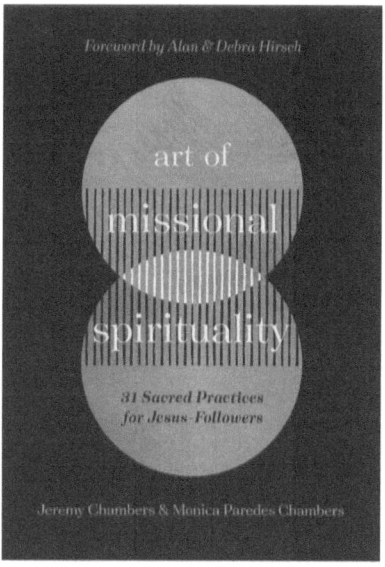

In an age of hyperactivity, spiritual superficiality, and a desperate scramble for quick fixes, this book beckons us into deeper waters—a missional life with God.

"*The missional lifestyle must be undergirded by a deep spirituality. Jeremy and Monica Chambers have created the perfect guide for developing these deep roots and provide accessible and actionable ideas for disciples of all levels of experience.*"
ANGIE WARD, PHD, director, Doctor of Ministry Program and associate professor of Leadership and Ministry, Denver Seminary; author, *Uncharted Leadership*

"*A fundamental guide for Christ-followers actively living on mission for Jesus. Jeremy and Monica have artfully curated thirty-one spiritual practices forged from their own missional living. These are the sacred practices that can bring harmony to our busy lives and deeper purpose in our work by helping us fall more deeply in love with Jesus.*"
BILL COUCHENOUR, director of deployment, Exponential; governing elder, Tampa Underground; coauthor, *Unleashed!*